Angus McDonald

Prophetic Numbers

The rise, progress and future destiny of the Mormons

Angus McDonald

Prophetic Numbers
The rise, progress and future destiny of the Mormons

ISBN/EAN: 9783337286491

Printed in Europe, USA, Canada, Australia, Japan

Cover: Foto ©Lupo / pixelio.de

More available books at **www.hansebooks.com**

PROPHETIC NUMBERS:

—OR—

THE RISE, PROGRESS AND FUTURE

DESTINY OF THE "MORMONS."

BY A FREE THINKING OPTICAL PROFESSOR,

Who will deliver lectures on the subject, illustrated by Stereoptican desolving views, and Zodiacal Map.

PUBLISHED BY W. M. EGAN,

SALT LAKE CITY,

1885.

	Page
Assassination of Joseph Smith	35
Bible doctrine	6-7
Book of Mormon and Bible in America	4
Celestial marriage	33, 71-72
Christopher Columbus	47
Church of Christ organized	29
Cleansing of the sanctuary	18
Destiny of the 'Mormons'	56
Discourse of Pres. Taylor	78
Early life of the author	7
Elder Brother	70
End of 1st woe	40
Extracts from B. of M.	64
Fulfilment of prophecy	21-58
Garden of Eden	30
Gentile nations to fall and rise no more	52
God appeared to Joseph Smith	28
God's time, angel's time	12
Great advance of arts, etc.	46
House of God to be set in order	42
Intelligence the glory of God	9
Jesus Christ a polygamist	60
Journey of the 'Mormons'	26
Johnson's Army	37
Keys to spiritual gifts	73
Man is an eternal being	8
Man-child taken unto God	20
Man-child's return to earth	27
Marriage of Virgin Mary	22
Martin Van Buren	32
Moroni appears to Joseph	28
Moses and Elias appear	31
New Jerusalem	30
Only Begotten of the Father	21
144,000 first borns	75
Order of Enoch revealed	39
Our relation to the U. S.	57
Power of the holy people to be scattered	53
Predictions of Daniel	10
Predicted destruction of American nations	76
Priesthood came through polygamy	63
Pres. Brigham Young	34
Pres. John Taylor	18, 39
Queen of heaven	77
Reign of the Judges typical of the United States	69
Revelations of St. John	26
Rule of the Dragon	24
Sealing power given	66
Song of Zion	50
Southern war	38
Table of prophetic numbers	14
10,000,000 of Indians	19
The three woes	47
The Spirit of the Lord on the Gentiles	68
The Sword of the Lord	52
War of Independence	67
Works of the Father	75
Zion of the Holy One	43
Zodiacal signs	73

INDEX, VOL. II.

	Page		Page
A Century cometh	155	Nucleus of truth	94
Age of First-born	89	Origin of the Gentiles	131
Angels	88	Ordination	99
Blind Horn	127	Order of Elijah	92
Center of Zion	114	Plotting destruction	154
Center of all Light	136	Priestcraft	146
Challenge	149	Prophetic Nmbers	80-160
Church of oneness	86	Rights of man	143
Church organized	96	Roman Power	125
Commands to Church	112	Sacrifice and faith	104
Controlers of the Zodiac	119	Salutation	98
Constitution of the U. S.	153	Salvation by gathering	152
Decree	122	Salvation, Esau Gentiles	109
Division of the Vision	121	Saving power	86
Duration and time	82	Seven Heads	83
Earth abides celestial law	97	Signs of the Numbers	84
Elijah the Prophet	115	Singular document	105
Everlasting order	107	Six Female Architects	118
False optical theory	132	Solar System	120
Family of Gods	135	Spirit eternal	141
Figure seven	126	Ten Horns	127
First-born	88	Testimony of John Taylor	100
First Covenant	129	" Geo. Q. Cannon	101
Fullness of my Gospel	95	" Jos. F. Smith	102
Gathering of mine Elect	111	" Jesus Christ	106
Gospel to Lamanites	91	Theocratic platform	81-129
Hypocrites	115	Three book salvation	150
Inquisitional test	90	Transgression	108
Kingdom of God	128	True Optics	137
Keys of salvation	142	Urim and Thummim	138
Labor	144	Vague speculations	134
Land monopoly	145	Visions	124
Limits of extension	152	Who is man	140
Messiah cut off	126	Woe to the Gentiles	110
Nimrod, first aristocracy	130	Words of a book	117

INTRODUCTORY.

THE Author was born in North Ouest Invernesshire Scotland, was sealed up unto eternal life in the Presbiterian Kirk when three months old; Recieved the rudiments of his education in the ancient Scotch language, called the Gaelic. In after life he fell from Grace and became a convert to Free Thought and a member of the Hall of Science in Glasgow.

In 1847, I became acquainted with a man calling himself an Elder of the Church of Jesus Christ of Latter-day Saints; after much controversy between him and me, he made the following bold declaration to me: "If you will submit your will to me and go by my council, I promise you in the name of Israel's God that the eyes of your understanding will be opened, and you shall know whence you came and where you are going and why you are here and the truth of the Bible will be revealed to you." To which I replied; Sir, I will take you at your word, and if I find what you say to be true, I will defend that power while I live; but, if I find it not true, I will expose the delusion with all the means in my reach.

Now, after a close investigation for 37 years, 29 of which I have been in Utah I do declare before God, angels and men, that the words of the Elder are true and his promise has been verified to me for which I am thankful. I know the Bible to be true in all its parts; It contains the words of the Gods, the words of angels, the words of devils, the words of men and, if you are very particular, the words of an ass. To me the Bible is the Key to Theology, the guage of Philosophy, the age of Reason and the Rights of man.

The Bible teaches that space and duration are boundless, that all things in space are endless, self-existing, male and female. The Bible teaches, that 144,000 self-luminous, self-existing men or Gods became brethern, the first born of the mothers, the only begotten of the Father.

By the optical laws embodied, the Theocratic order of Government, viz. many females to one male, is eternal life;—thus a plurality of wives, a plurality of births, deaths and resurrections all nature becomes a unit; all power is confered in one. These eternal self-luminous men take flesh upon them by and of their own free will, by parental law, that they themselves may exercise the creative power.

The negative of this is also true; by the optical laws embodied in an Aristocratic Government of permiting many males to one female, is eternal death.

The naturalist, by a single bone, will describe the kind of animal; the physiognomist by the sight of a hand will describe the person; the phrenologist by the sight of the head will describe the character; the mind reader by a single hair will describe the temper; a touch on any part of the body is felt by the whole body; a single wave of air if not interfered with will extend into infinitude. In proof of which see the following.

"God standeth in the congregation of the mighty; he judgeth among the gods. How long will ye judge unjustly, and accept the persons of the wicked? Selah. Defend the poor and fatherless; do justice to the afflicted and needy. Deliver the poor and needy; rid them out of the hand of the wicked. They know not neither will they understand; they walk on in darkness: all the foundations of the earth are out of course. I have said, Ye are gods; and all of you are children of the Most High. But ye shall die like men, and fall like one of the princes. Arise, O God, judge the earth; for thou shalt inherit all nations." Psalm 82.

"Keep not thou silence, O God: hold not thy peace, and be not still, O God. For, lo, thine enemies make a tumult; and they that hate thee have lifted up the head. They have taken crafty council against thy people, and consulted against thy hidden ones. They have said, Come, and let us cut them off from being a nation; that the name of Israel may be no more in remembrance. For they have consulted together with one consent: they are confederate against thee." . . . .

"Who said let us take to ourselves the houses of God in possession. O my God make them like a wheel; as the stubble before the wind. As the fire burneth a wood, and as the flame setteth the mountains on fire; so persecute them with thy tempest and make them afraid with thy storm. Fill their faces with shame; that they may seek thy name O, Lord. Let them be confounded and troubled for ever; yea, let them be put to shame, and perish; that men may know that thou, whose name alone is JEHOVAH, art the Most High over all the earth."

"I will hear what God the Lord will speak: for he will speak peace unto his people, and to his saints; but let them not turn again unto folly. Surely his salvation is nigh them that fear him; that glory may dwell in our land. Mercy and truth are met together; righteousness and peace have kissed each other. Truth shall spring out of the earth; and righteousness shall look down from heaven. Yea, the Lord shall give that which is good; and our land shall yield her increase." Psalm 85.

"And now, verily I say unto you, I was in the beginning with the Father, and am the first born; and all those who are begotten through me are partakers of the glory of the same, and are the church of the first born. Ye were also in the beginning with the Father; that which is Spirit, even the Spirit of truth, and truth is knowledge of things as they are, and as they were, and as they are to come; and whatsoever is more or less than this, is the spirit of that wicked one, who was a liar from the beginning. The spirit of truth is of God. I am the spirit of truth, and John bore record of me, saying—he received a fullness of truth, yea, even of all truth, and no man recieveth a fulness unless he keepeth his commandments. He that keepeth his commandments recieveth truth and light, until he is glorified in truth and knoweth all things.

"Man was also in the beginning with God. Intelligence, or the light of truth, was not created or made, neither indeed can be. All truth is independent in that sphere in which God has placed it, to act for itself, as all intelligence also, otherwise there is no existence. Behold, here is the agency of man, and here is the condemnation of man, because that which was from the beginning is plainly manifest unto them, and they receive not the light. And every man that recieveth not the light is under condemnation, for man is spirit. The elements are eternal, and spirit and element, inseperably connected, recieveth a fulness of joy; and when separated, man cannot recieve a fulness of joy. The elements are the tabernacle of God; yea, man is the tabernacle of God, even temples; and whatsoever temple is defiled, God shall destroy that temple.

"The glory of God is intelligence, or, in other words, light and truth; light and truth forsaketh that evil one. Every spirit of man was innocent in the beginning, and God having redeemed man from the fall, men became again in their infant state, innocent before God. And that wicked one cometh and taketh away light and truth; but verily I say unto you, my servant Frederic G. Williams, you have continued under this condemnation; you have not taught your children light and truth, according to the commandments, and that wicked one hath power, as yet, over you, and this is the cause of your affliction. And now a commandment I give unto you, if you will be delivered, you shall set in order your own house, for there are many things that are not right in your house.

Verily, I say unto my servant Sidney Rigdon, that in some things he hath not kept the commandments concerning his children; therefore, firstly set in order thy house.

Verily, I say unto you my servant Joseph Smith, jun., or in other words, I will call you friends, for you are my friends, and ye shall have an inheritance with me. I called you servants for the world's sake, and ye are their servants for my sake; and now, verily I say unto Joseph Smith, jun., you have not kept the commandments, and must needs stand rebuked before the Lord. Your family must needs repent and forsake some things, and give more earnest heed unto your sayings, or be removed out of their place. What I say unto one, I say unto all; pray always lest that wicked one have power in you and remove you out of your place." Doc. and Cov. Sec. 93.

"We occupy to-day a very peculiar position and it is proper that we, as Latter-day Saints, should comprehend that position and our various responsibilities in relation to the world in which we live, the nation with which we are associated, and the duties and responsibilities which devolve upon us as messengers of salvation to proclaim the Gospel to mankind. It is further necessary that we should comprehend the past, that we should comprehend the present, and that we should also—under the influence and by the direction of the Spirit of the living God—comprehend the things of the future; for we, as Latter-day Saints, have to do with the past, we have to do with the present, and we have to do with the future." *Des. News*, Oct. 27, '83.

PROPHETIC NUMBERS;

—OR—

The Rise, Progress and Future

DESTINY OF THE "MORMONS."

CHAPTER I.

Prophetic Numbers—Periods and eras—Daniel and Revelations made plain—Joseph Smith the prophet; his birth, life and death etc.

FROM every century, commencing with the 6th century before the birth of Christ, in which century the prophet Daniel lived, have we had different theories and views of eminent men, who have endeavored to interpret the writings of Daniel and John the Revelator. Especially have they insisted upon locating the beginning and ending of certain prophetic periods of time, and in their arrangement have conformed to the same to suit historical events consistent with their own peculiar views.

The author of this article, with respectful consideration for their intended honesty of purpose and desire to fathom the misterious writings mentioned, questions their authenticity and correctness, and for the information of the reader as well as his criticism submits the following important prophetic periods of time, or eras, refered to in Daniel, Revelations and by the prophet Joseph Smith, to his inspection:

Our prophetic figures, constituting weeks, months and years, which are the periods of time in which certain events are prophecied of, will be arranged in the order of their fulfillment. The rule of measurement is; *first*, by the command of God; *second*, by the example of Jacob; *third*, by the fulfillment of the 62 weeks to the death of the Messiah. See Num. 13, Gen. 29: 20-29, and Dan. 9

"Seventy weeks are determined upon thy people and upon thy holy city, to finish the transgression, and to make an end of sins, and to make reconciliation for iniquity, and to bring in everlasting righteousness, and to seal up the vision and prophecy, and to anoint the most Holy. Know therefore and understand, that from the going forth of the commandment to restore and to build Jerusalem, unto the Messiah the prince, shall be seven weeks, and three score and two weeks: the street thall be built again, and the wall, even in troublous times:" Dan. 9: 24-25.

The establishing of a prophetic starting point has baffled every known writer upon the book of Daniel and Revelations;* hence, its importance.

The Author therefore proposes to give the Key, which will unlock the entire prophetic numbers relating to the subject treated upon, reaching over a period from 600 years B. C. to the 20th century or 1945, A. D.

These prophetic periods of years will be divided into DIVISION PERIODS and will constitute the entire number of years as given by the Angel Gabriel to Daniel, namely; 2300 years. These years therefore are symbolized in some instances, but in others

---

* The author has no reference to those who have writen upon those books of the Bible under the spirit of inspiration, or by the gift of the Holy Ghost, as has been revealed through the prophet Joseph Smith.

by a defined given time. The important position taken by the writer in the interpretation of these prophetic numbers was brought about by his reflections upon the mission of the prophet Joseph Smith, and the more he thought upon the matter, the more thoroughly convinced did he become, that the birth of Joseph Smith, on the 23rd of December 1805, was prophetic upon mathematical, astronomical and Bible numerical calculations, and, after much labor, the key to these three considerations was found, and the importance of the subject became more impressive. In the treatment of the subject, *Prophetic Numbers*, in this volume, the mathematical Bible key only is given, but to confirm the matter of the true prophetic starting point, the book of Mormon will be refered to.

With these preliminaries, our subject will, to be properly understood, open with a table of numerical considerations, and as historians have undertook to define what is angel's time, man's time and God's time, I will refer the reader to the following quotations upon the matter, as it is from the same that the author has made his deductions, because the true key to unlock the misterious book of Daniel could only here be found.

The things of God must be considered through the proper channel, the gift of the Holy Ghost, by direct revelation and inspiration, for there is a spirit in man and the inspiration of the Almighty giveth it understanding. By this we are led to interpret the Scriptures.

"And I, Abraham, had the Urim and Thummim, which the Lord my God had given unto me, in Ur of the Chaldees; and I saw the stars, that they were very great, and that one of them was nearest unto the throne of God; and there were many great ones which were near unto it; and the Lord said unto me, These are the governing ones; and the name of the great one is *Kolob*, because it is near unto me, for I am the Lord thy God; I have set this one to govern all those which belong to the same order of that upon which thou standest. And the Lord said unto me, by the Urim and Thummim, that Kolob was after the manner of the Lord, according to its times and seasons in the revolutions thereof, that one revolution was a day unto the Lord, after his manner of reckoning, it being one thousand years according to the time appointed to that whereon thou standest. This is the reckoning of the Lords time, according to the reckoning of Kolob." Book of Abraham, P. of G. P. page 30.

"In answer to the question, 'Is not the reckoning of God's time, angel's time, prophet's time and man's time according to the planet on which they reside?' I answer yes. But there are no angels who minister to this earth but those who do belong or have belonged to it." Doc. & Cov. Sec. 130.

There are still other quotations that could be given, but the above answers our purpose.

The reader will understand our subject by keeping in mind this fact; that our period of years will be symbolized by a *chain*, each prophetic numerical period being a link for a year.

One thousand of our years is one day with the Lord; hence, one hour with the Lord is 41 years and 8 months.

PROBLM I.

1000 years ÷ 24 hours = 41 years 8 months.

The angel's time, times and half-time is, when reckoned after the Lord's time, 1260 years, and when reckoned after man's time $3\frac{1}{2}$ years.

PROBLEM 2.
After Angel's time: Time, 360 years,
(plural) Times, 720 "
Half a time, 180 " = 1260.

PROBLEM 3.
After man's time; Time, 360 days,
(plural) Times, 720 "
Half a time, 180 " = 1260 days.
which are 3 years and a half.

All reckoning of time is upon the cycle of degrees
viz., 360 days to the year, or
12 months to the year, and
30 days to the month.

TABLE OF PROPHETIC NUMBERS.

The *First Chain* of 434 years or links are the 62 weeks of the angel's time given to Daniel 9; 25, commencing with the going forth of the "decree" of the King of Persia, Artaxerxes to Nehemiah to rebuild the walls of Jerusalem to the Crucifixion of our Lord Jesus Christ. . . . **434**

The *Second Chain* of 49 years or links, are the 7 weeks of the angel's time given to Daniel 9; 25, comencing with the Crucifixion and reaches to the destruction of Jerusalem. The prince refered to in the passage was Titus the son of Vespacian, Emperor of the Roman Empire, the 4th diverse Beast in the vision of the 4 beasts, Dan. 7. The destruction of Jerusalem took place 49 years or 7 weeks after the Crucifixion. **49**

The *Third Chain* of 495 years or links are the 70 weeks Dan. 9; 24, and half a week, Dan. 9; 27, of the angels time, commencing with the destruction of Jerusalem unto the going of the woman (or church) into the wilderness. **495**

In connection with this important date; namely, 544 years after the crucifixion, must be considered the years given to John the Revelator by the angel who reckoned time to him and informed John that from the taking up of the man-child unto God and the going of the woman into the wilderness was to be 1260 years before the same was to be restored again to the earth, Rev. 12; 5-6. This, therefore, when added to the 544 years would make 1804 years after the death of the Messiah as the end of the fourth chain of years.

The 1290 years given to Daniel by the angel begin before the 1260 years with the taking up of the man-child (or priesthood) unto God, or when the last of the priesthood was destroyed and "the abomination that maketh desolate set up," Dan. 12; 11, and end with the restitution, agreeing with and including John's 1260 years, but as it commences 30 years previous it shows that the man-child was taken up unto God 30 years before the woman was driven into the wilderness. Agreeable to John's time and Dan. 12; 7, therefore, the man-child should be born again after the 1260 years were completed and 30 years before the return of the woman from the wilderness. We therefore take, for the *Fourth Chain*, the 1260 years or links, commencing with the going of the woman into the wilderness and end with her return. **1260**

To make these dates more plain we introduce the following diagram:

```
              1290 days or years of Dan 12: 11.
  _____   ___
 |  |       | 1260 years Rev 12; 5-6. |       |   |
 |D |       |                         |       |   |
 |e |  30   | Woman in wilderness.    |       |Res|
 |a |years  |                         |       |tor|
 |t |       |                         |  30   |ati|
 |h |       |                         | years |on.|
 |  |       | birth of man-child.     |       |   |
  ‾‾‾‾‾‾‾‾‾‾‾‾‾‾‾‾‾‾‾‾‾‾‾‾‾‾‾‾‾‾‾‾‾‾‾‾‾‾‾‾‾‾‾   ‾‾‾
              1260 y. to birth of man-child.
```

The first 1260 years commences with the death of the man-child and ends with the birth of the man-child Joseph Smith, Dec. 23, 1805, A. D. The second 1260 years commences with our former prophetic date of the woman going into the wilderness and ends with the restoration of the woman with all her priestly power in 1835, A. D. The latter 30 years are indeed prophetic years and are considered in the subject matter to follow.

The *Fifth Chain* of 45 years or links begin with the year 1835, which also is the beginning of the prophet Joseph Smith's 56 prophetic years or links. These 45 years or links are the last 45 years of the angel's time of 1335 years and when added to the 1290 years make the 1335 years, for after the angel had given to the prophet Daniel this time, 1290 years, the angel thus addressed him: "Blessed is he that waiteth and cometh to the one thousand three hundred thirty and five days," or years, Dan. 12; 12-13. It is quite evident then, that these 45 years are the continuation of the 1290 years and end with 1879, A. D. This is important, and the reader will bear in mind this date or the end of the angel's time to Daniel 1335 years, for "blessed is he that wateth and cometh" and *understandeth* the end of the 1335 years.

A. D. 1880 finds Pres. John Taylor, the 2nd successor of the prophet Joseph Smith in the Presidency over the Church of Jesus Christ of Latter-days, and the ending of these 45 years in 1879, constitutes the first division of our table of prophetic numbers.

Total footings,

45
2283

We now number from the 1st year of the reign of Zedekiah.

This table will constitute, in its entirety, a chain of years, reaching from 600 B. C. to 1945, A. D.

	YEARS or LINKS.
The *first chain* of 200 years, or links, commences with the first year of the reign of Zedekiah; in which year Lehi left Jerusalem for the promised land, America.	200
From rebuilding of wall to death of the Messiah.	434
From death of Messiah to the overthrow of the Jews and destruction of Jerusalem.	49
From destruction of Jerusalem to the going of the church into the wilderness.	495
From the going of the church into the wilderness to the restoration.	1260
From the restoration unto the end of Daniel's time 1335, as given by the angel.	45

This ends the chain of years from the 1st year of the reign of Zedekiah to the year of our Lord 1879, when Pres. John Taylor commences to preside in the 1st year of the remaining years or links, which will complete the Angel Gabriel's time, given in the 8th chapter of Daniel, as the entire period of time from the commencement to rebuild the walls of Jerusalem unto the cleansing of the Sanctuary, which taketh place at the end of these 2300 years, or in the year 1896.

Total years from 1st year of Zedekiah, | 2483

As our reckoning is from the rebuilding of the walls of Jerusalem; namely, the time given by the Angel Gabriel we deduct the 200 years from the 1st year of the reign of Zedekiah, | 200

which leaves as part of the 2300 years, | 2283

It will be seen that this brings us to the year 1880, A. D., and leaves yet, 17 years, or links, to make up the 2300 years, or links, of the Angel Gabriel's time. This ends the first division of our prophetic table of numbers.

SECOND DIVISION.

This division will include four departments as follows:

First, the 56 years of the prophet Joseph Smith.
Second, the 70 years of the prophet Jeremiah.
Third, the 1st, 2nd and 3rd woes or hours.
Fourth, the 17 years, or last links of the angel's time of 2300 years, which are the links, or years of the Ancient of days' time. Explained in the subject matter that follows.

The 56 years of the prophet Joseph Smith commence with the year 1835, and end in 1891, and is also explained in the subject matter.

The 70 years, or links of the prophet Jeremiah's chain of prophetic numbers, commences with the sounding of the gospel trump by the going forth of the 12 apostles unto the world, and therefore commences with the year 1835, A. D., and end in the year 1904, this being the period of God's mercy unto the Gentiles before the commencement of the 3rd woe, or hour, in 1905.

The 1st woe, or hour, commenced in 1820, A. D. which was the year the Father and Son appeared to Joseph Smith, and ends in 1862.

The 2nd woe commenced in 1862, and ends 1904.

The 3rd woe, which will be cut short, however, commences in 1905, it being the period in which the Ancient of Days in person will set upon his throne to judge the nations. It is explained in the subject matter. These 3 woes are each 41 years and 8 months long

The 17 years are the links of the presidency of Pres. John Taylor and are the last 17 links of the Angel Gabriel's time given to Daniel, and end in 1896. The chain of 17 links commencing in 1879, is a highly important division of the 2300 years, and are years of profound reflection, which will be considered at length in the subject matter.

Please note that the taking of the man-child unto God, referred to by John the Revelator, is men who held the higher Melchisedek Priesthood, being killed, or taken unto God through the gate of the martyr; the Aaronic Priesthood remaining 30 years. The table on next page is condencely arranged.

Our Prophetic Table being now complete we enter the consideration of these dates, and surround them with evidences that will cause the reflecting mind to pause before pronouncing against the position taken.

Prophetic Numbers,

DIVIDED INTO WEEKS, DAYS AND WOES OR YEARS

The **2300** days commense **400** B. C

TABLE OF WEEKS.

A. D.	Weeks.	Days in week.		Date of Vision
34	62	×	7*	= 434
83	7	×	7	= 49
574	70½	×	7	= 495
574	139½	×	7	= 978
30†	62	×	7	= 434
544	77½	×	7	= 544

TABLE OF DAYS.

A. D.		Days.		A. D.		Date of Vision.
544	+	1260	=	1804	=	2208
570	+	1260	=	1830	=	2234
544	+	1290	=	1834	=	2238
544	+	1335	=	1879	=	2283
978‡	+	1260	+	45 + 17§	=	2300

TABLE OF WOES AND YEARS.

A. D.		Woes and years.		A. D.
1820	+	42	=	1862
1862	+	42	=	1904
1904	+	41	=	1945
1835	+	56	=	1891
1835	+	70	=	1905
1845	+	100	=	1945

* The authority for reducing weeks to days and using a day for a year is: 1st, by the command of God, Num. 14: 34; 2nd, by the example of Jacob, Gen. 29: 27; 3rd, by the fulfillment of the 62 weeks, Dan. 9: 26.
† See Page 15-18, this work. ‡ Date of Vision to end of weeks. § See this work page 18-19.

CHAPTER II.

The Only Begotten—7 weeks—70 weeks etc.—Daniel's and John's dates—Restoration—New Jerusalem—America—Persecution and war—Presidency—The Woes—Star of Bethlehem—3½ years to 1891.

THE 62 weeks, or 434 years, constitute some important events, the greatest of which might be considered the birth of the Messiah, the Only Begotten of the Father.

The many conflicting views, theories and explainations which have been given in regard to the character of the Savior, His birth, death and mission on earth, necessitates the introduction of matter explanatory of the same conforming to the prophetic numbers given.

The signification of the term, Only Begotten of the Father, is embodied in the following: Jesus Christ the Son of God was begotten by the Father as you and I were begotten, and being the only begotten implies that the Father of our Lord Jesus Christ did not beget other children by His wife, the mother of Jesus.* Now when Joseph the betrothed

---

* That is to say, by the same mother during the mortality of her life, or during her natural life-time in the flesh, for the reason that Jesus, being the redeemer of the world, and being born of the woman upon this the lowest of the creations of God, all the inhabitants of the Universe, circumscribed by the covenant, are made the recipients of the salvation that comes by the shedding the blood of the Son of God at the crucifixion. Of all the inhabited worlds,

husband of Mary understood from the angel Gabriel that Mary, by the interposition of the Almighty, was with child, and he commanded to take Mary for his wife, but knew her not until the Holy Child was born and weaned.

As regards the marriage of Mary with the Father of Jesus we find important information given in Luke 1.* It therefore being established that God himself came down upon the earth and had Mary for His wife and on His return to the heavens, gave

---

this is the only one that would put the Lord Jesus Christ to death. Therfore in this world and among her inhabitants we have gods, angels, terrestial and telestial beings, the earth being the turning point; hence, Christ descended below all things that he might rise above all things, and many of his bretheren, partaking of the glory of the Father descended likewise to be his assistants.

* "I am he who was prepared from the founhation of the world to redeem my people. Behold I am Jesus Christ. I am the Father and the Son. In me shall all mankind have light and that eternally, even they who shall belive on my name; and they shall become my sons and my daughters. And never have I showed myself unto man whom I have created, for never has man believed in me as thou hast. Seest thou that ye are created after mine own image? Yea, even all men were created in the beginning, after mine own image. Behold, this body, which ye now behold, is the body of my spirit; and man have I created after the body of my spirit; and even as I appear unto thee to be in the spirit, will I appear unto my people in the flesh." Ether, B. of M.

"And now Abinadah said unto them, I would that ye should understand that God himself shall come down among the children of men, and shall redeem his people; and because he dwelleth in the flesh, he shall be called the Son of God: and having subjected the flesh to the will of the Father, being the Father and the Son; the Father because he was conceived by the power of God; and the Son, because of the flesh; thus becoming the Father and Son: and they are one God, yea, the very eternal Father of heaven and of earth; and thus the flesh becoming subject to the Spirit, or the Son to the Father, being one God, suffereth temptation, and yieldeth not to the temptation, but suffereth himself to be mocked, and scourged, and cast out, and disowned by his people." Record of Zeniff. Mosiah.

her to Joseph, who raised up seed unto the Lord, for Mary had several children by Joseph. In this we see how God himself conformed to the law which was given, and which is understood to-day, that when a man dies, who has a wife, or wives, married to him for time and eternity, that the children born are to him, whomsoever may marry his wives after his death. When Jesus was about to expire he turned his eyes upon John, his beloved deciple, who stood close by the cross and thus addressed him; "Behold thy mother. And from that hour that deciple took her unto his own home." See John 19; 25-27.

The offering unto Jesus, of a spunge of vinegar mingled with oil on the plant called hissop, a highly aromatic herb, constitutes the offering denominated in the Holy Scriptures, an offering for sin,* which when performed, it being the last great act, Jesus gave up the Ghost, and the 62 weeks were fulfilled, the Messiah being cut off.

We now consider the period of 7 weeks, or 49 years, that were to intervene between the death of the Savior and the destruction of the temple and city of Jerusalem.

"And the people of the prince that shall come shall destroy the city and the sanctuary; and the end thereof shall be with a flood, and unto the end of the war desolations are determined." Dan. 9; 26. This prince refered to was Titus the son of the Emperor Vespasian. The ending of the 7 weeks, or overthrow of Jerusalem took place in the 79th year of the Christian Era.†

The 62 weeks or 434 years, and the 7 weeks or

---

* Isaiah 53; 10. There have been other interpretations.

† Historians have generally given the year 70 A. D., as the period of the overthrow of the Jews, but there are differnces, and we therefore take the prophetic period.

49 years are the first 483 years of the 2300 years of Daniel, which commenced at the decree to rebuild the walls of Jerusalem 200 years after Lehi left for America.*

The next prophetic period of the 2300 years is the time circumscribed by the era of 490 years or 70 weeks, which constitutes time commencing with the destruction of Jerusalem by the Roman prince, Titus, unto the going of the woman into the wilderness.

Having established a defined prophetic date; namely, the death of the Messiah, we locate without contradiction, the beginning of the era, when the Church of Christ in former days, or the woman, should go into the wilderness. Our date therefore brings us to the year which completed the entire overthrow of the entire delegated authority of the priesthood, and the last ordinance of the true Church ceased to be performed and christian Rome verged into and under the dominion of pagan Rome in fullfillment of the prophetic import of the vision, and the Dragon enters upon his rule, having prevailed against the saints and overcame the Church of Christ and established an apostate priesthood.

* The importance of the matter of this decree involves the consideration of our first prophetic year, which, when established, our great subject is correctly followed and the seeker after truth is not led astray. The labor and patient study of these important events has extended over many years. The signing of the decree by Artaxerxes, King of Persia, took place in the month Nisan (part of our April) in the 20th year of his reign. Historians have confounded this decree to Nehemiah, with the former decree to Esdra, or Ezra; hence, have given a wrong date to the beginning of the 62 weeks of Daniel, which realy commence in the same year that the decree was given, for Nehemiah immediately repaired to Jerusalem and, after three days, there commenced to rebuild the wall of Jerusalem and the gates of the city. See Ezra 7, and Nehemiah 2. The true time being 400 years B. C.

This going of the church into the wilderness, or obscurity, was for a defined period covered by the number of prophetic years considered further on.

To make our prophetic numbers plain and comprehensive, we now compute the time, from the rebuilding of the walls of Jerusalem to the going of the church into the wilderness.

To the death of the Messiah are 62 weeks or 434 years. The age of the Savior being correctly given in the Book of Mormon, we are enabled to locate the exact day when these 62 weeks ended, both as to the Jewish reckoning and A. D. reckoning; this will be given when we consider the year that the church came out of the wilderness.

To the destruction of Jerusalem are 7 weeks, 49 years. These are part of the seven weeks and three score and two weeks, Dan. 9; 25.

To the going of the woman into the wilderness are 70 weeks and $\frac{1}{2}$ a week or the largest half of the week in the midst of the week, 5 years Dan. 9: 20, making $70\frac{1}{2}$ weeks or including largest $\frac{1}{2}$ week 495 years, bringing us to 544* after the crucifixion.

The period then from the rebuilding of the walls of Jerusalem to the rule of the Dragon, or going of the church into the wilderness comprises 978 years of the 2300, or to date in the Christian Era period, 574 A. D.

* As our Savior was born in the year 4 Anno Domini date, according to Cruden's Concordance and other works, this date would be 574 A. D. In a work now published entitled "Prophetic History and the Fulfillment of prophecy from 600 years B. C. to A. D. 1891," the date 570 is given as the time the church went into the wilderness. This date 570 A. D. being surrounded with such strong historical evidence is accepted as the date when the church was disorganized, and 574 as the date when complete obscurity settled upon the church. The re-organization took place in 1830 just 1260 years after the disorganization, and the complete organization perfected with power in 1835.

SECOND DIVISION.

John the Revelator has laid before him in vision the fearful scenes which fill up the dark period following down the stream of events; when the earth was without the true church, and that there might be no mistake made in the proper chronological data, he is given to understand that the church was to be in the wilderness 1260 years, and 1260 years was to pass before the man-child was to be again restored to the earth, or to plainly state the matter, 1260 years was to complete the period of time that darkness should reign.

The period of the going of the woman into the wilderness, or 574 A. D. with the years of John added therefore completes the prophetic chain to the year of our Lord 1834.

From the evidence which lies before us in Daniel and his 1290 years we conform to the symbolical arrangement, and as Daniel's time of 1290 years ends at the same time as John's time of 1260 years, therefore it must have commenced some 30 years previous. It is found by both Daniel's and John's writings that there must have been a time intervening between the taking up of the man-child unto God, (or the killing of the men of the high priesthood) and the going of the woman into the wilderness. Daniel evidently saw from the date of the former to the end, while John saw from the date of the latter to the same end of darkness and restoration of power. The difference in the two periods, therefore, shows that the man-child was taken unto God 30 years before the woman was driven into the wilderness. As the man-child was evidently taken away 30 years before the apostasy we might well look for the birth of the man-child again 30 years before the restoration of all the keys and powers.

From the death of the man-child to the end of the 1260 years would close a chain in 1804, and the 1st link of the next prophetic chain of 30 years to the "end of these things," commences with 1805, in which link or year, according to the fullfillment of the prophetic revelations or periods of the visions of Daniel and John there must occur an event in conformity to the years above mentioned.

On the 23rd day of December 1805, in the territory circumscribed by the geographical outlines of the possessions of the Government of the United States of America, and in the State of Vermont, there was born a *man-child*, and the same is he, who, according to the Book of Mormon and the Bible, was named after his illustrious ancestor, Joseph of Egypt, as well as the name of his father, he was christened and named *Joseph Smith jun.*

This prophetic chain beginning in 1805, constitutes 30 links or years, and is the last 30 years of Daniel's 1290 years, which commenced with the year of our Lord 545, for Daniel and John were informed of the same matter with this difference; Daniel was shown what would take place during a period of 2300 years, divided into weeks and years, as has been shown, and notably the 30 and 45 years or links which added to the 1260 are Daniel's 1335 years.

First to be treated upon are the 30 years beginning with the year 1805, A. D. These 30 years are of vital importance to the children of men. Almost the entire list of Bible prophets had their minds opened to the culminating events of this period, the first of which is surrounded with so much interesting matter it becomes necessary to refer to the most important prophetic year of these 30 referred to, which is the 16th, or classifying the period proper, the year 1820, A. D. In this year Joseph Smith, the father of Joseph the seer, resided in the town of Manchester, Ontario Co., N. Y., having removed from Vermont to Palmira and then to Manchester. The boy Joseph, being at this time in his 15th year.

The extraordinary wave of religious excitment which was then sweeping over the sea of humanity, found its advocates in the family of Joseph, he being influenced by the excitement and by positions taken by some of his brethers, sisters and friends, was induced to give his attention to the investigation of the plan of salvation and the importance of a preparation for a future state of existence. To come at an understanding he carried out the plan recorded in the Epistle of James: "If any of you lack wisdom let him ask of God, who giveth to all men liberally and upbraideth not, and it shall be given him."

On repairing to a grove, close by his father's house, for the purpose of praying to God for guidance in the matter, he was immediately beset by the power of darkness, but on lifting up his voice unto God, the heavens opened and God, the Eternal Father, and His Only Begotten Son, Jesus Christ, stood before him. For which see "Items of Church History," "Gift of the Holy Ghost" etc., published in pamphlet form, being extracts from the "History of Joseph Smith the Prophet."

The next great prophetic year of the 30 in which great events take place, is the 19th, or 1823, A. D. On the night of the 21st of September of this year, Joseph on repairing to his room to retire for the night, knelt down in humble prayer. Soon the glory of God illuminated the room, and a Holy Angel appeared before him. The information imparted to him by the Holy Angel, whose name was Moroni, gave Joseph to understand that the time was near for the restoration of the fullness of the Gospel which was recorded upon the golden plates, and which were hid up in a hill near by, and which in the due time of the Lord was to come forth; and that he, Joseph Smith, had been chosen the instrument in the hands of the Almighty to bring about the restoration of the Gospel, and the establishing of the true and legitimate Church of God. This was fulfilled on the morning of the 22nd of September, 1827, A. D., which is the 23rd year of the prophetic 30. In this year the golden plates, containing the fullness of the Gospel of Christ to Gentile and to Jew, was delivered to Joseph Smith by this same Holy Angel. This was the Book of Mormon. Our next important year of the 30 is the 26th, or 1830, A. D.

This year, on the 6th day of the Jewish month ABIB or NISAN, which falls in our April, the Church of Jesus Christ of Latter-days was organized by and through the commands of Jesus Christ, the authority of the Holy Priesthood having been previously conferred upon Joseph Smith and Oliver Cowdery--- the Aaronic,* or Levitical, by John the Baptist and the Melchisedek, or higher priesthood, by Peter, James and John.

---

* Words of the Angel, John, (the Baptist) spoken to Joseph Smith, Jr., and Oliver Cowdery, as he (the angel) laid his hands upon their heads and ordained them to the Aaronic Priesthood, in Harmony, Susquehanna County, Pennsylvania. May 15th, 1829.

Upon you, my fellow servants, in the name of Messiah, I confer the Priesthood of Aaron, which holds the keys of the ministering of angels, and of the gospel of repentance, and of baptism by immersion for the remission of sins; and this shall never be taken again from the earth, until the sons of Levi do offer again an offering unto the Lord in righteousness.

The higher priesthood was given some time between May and June 1829. See D. & C. Sec. 18-20.

Our next consideration is the 27th of the prophetic 30 years, or 1831, A. D. In no history of which the 19th century's library gives us a catalogue can be found information which imparts to us the knowledge where is located the land which was termed the Garden of Eden, or the place where Adam or Michael first took up his place of residence, and where he gave names unto all the animals and where he was permitted to first see the glorious mirrored beauty of his wife, "our Mother Eve," reflected upon the silvered waters of the paradistic home. In a revelation given to Joseph the Seer in July, 1831, in Missouri, this land or garden is revealed, and Independence, Jackson Co., Missouri, is the place or centre constituting the capitol of Idumea, or the place of the Holy City of the Bible and Book of Mormon, and called the *New Jerusalem*.

Our next consideration is the 30th or last year of 30 prophetic links or years, which end in 1834. This last year witnessed the departure of the Saints from Jackson Co. Missouri, having been driven from the great centre where the Capitol City, Zion, is to be built, which still is and for yet a little season will remain in possession of the enemy, and in fulfillment of the predictions of the prophets is trodden by the feet of the Gentiles.

We now consider the prophetic 45 years, which commence with the year 1835. These 45 years or links are the last 45 years of the prophet Daniel's 1335 years, and are also part of the prophet Joseph Smith's 56 years, which also commence with the year 1835. These years are intencely interesting and prophetic. The 1st link or year witnessed the organization of the Twelve Apostles and the two

Quorums of Seventies, completing the organization of the church 1260 years after its prophecied total destruction.

The 2nd year 1836, the Kirtland Temple was dedicated, on the 27th of March.* On the 3rd day of April following, the Lord appeared unto Joseph Smith and Oliver Cowdery, there also appeared Moses, Elias, and Elijah, and many holy angels and prophets, and the glory of God surrounded the temple, within and without the power of God was made manifest.

In the 3rd year, 1837, the English Mission was opened and the far off land, where ruled the 10 kingdoms or prophetic horns of the 4th diverse or Roman Beast, resounded with the Gospel Trump.

In the 4th year, 1838, Joseph Smith, the Seer,

---

*VISIONS AND MANIFESTATIONS IN THE KIRTLAND TEMPLE.—"*But as Paul said, so say I, let us come to visions and revelations.*"—On the evening of the 21st of Jan. 1836, after annointing and blessing father Smith, the 12 and first presidency being present, the heavens were opened and the prophet Joseph beheld the celestial Kingdom of God.

"I saw the transcendent beauty of the gate through which the heirs of that kingdom will enter, which was like unto circling flames of fire. Also the blazing throne of God. I saw father Adam, Abraham, and my father and mother, and my brother Alvin that had long since slept... Angels ministered unto them (those present) as well as to myself..... The house was filled with the glory of God."

Some saw the face of the Savior. Holy angels administered unto many. The spirit of prophecy and revelation was poured out with mighty power. Friday Jan. 22nd the gift of tongues fell upon many in mighty power and the holy angels mingled their voices with those present. Thursday, Jan 28th, on the sealing of the blessings, which had been pronounced upon the heads of the first 7 presidents of the 1st seventy by Pres. Rigdon, Elder Roger Orton saw a mighty angel riding upon a horse of fire with a flaming sword in his hand, followed by five others, encircling the house to protect the saints, even the Lord's annointed, from the power of Saten. Many others beheld the glorious hevenly hosts, and others, wonderful visions,—*History of Joseph Smith.*

the Servant refered to in the parable of the vinyard in the Book of Mormon, the head of this last dispensation, the dispensation of the fulness of times, was betrayed into the hands of the Gentiles and sentenced to be shot, but by a division in the tribunal escaped the death penalty. Joseph Smith could not have sealed his testimony with his blood until 1844, because of the events which prophetically marked out the number of links of the chain of his life.

In the 5th year, 1839, the typical Roman Pilate, in the character of Martin Van Buren, presided over the United States of America, upon the escutcheons or banners of whom are written *Freedom and Equal Rights*. The national ensign, the Stars and Stripes, ever unfurled to the breeze, stands, the proud memorial of a free and independent nation, inviting all nations, independent of cast, color or religion, to partake of the enjoyment of those equal rights, *Life Liberty and the persuit of Happiness*. With such a national supremacy, Joseph Smith, whose ancestors bravely fought to establish this free and independent nation, as a son of the prophetic republic. repaired to the Capital City of Washington, and with a noble true and godlike mein, in language touching and pathetic begged for redress, but alas! the withering touch which ruffled the feathers of the American Eagle which will result in its being entirely plucked, was yet reserved for Martin Van Buren who did but say unto Joseph's humble and pleading appeal,

"Your cause is just, but I can do nothing for you."

We pass the 6th year, or 1840 A. D., and consider the 7th, or 1841 A. D. In this year, on the 19th day of January, Joseph the Seer received a command to build a house unto the Lord, and the Temple at Nauvoo was commenced.

In the 8th year, 1842 A. D., Joseph Smith the Seer writes unto the Church that most important and highly interesting address reviewing the great prophetic events since the coming forth of the Book of Mormon, as also the ordinance of baptism for the dead, and other important keys.

In the 9th year, 1843 A. D., Joseph Smith the Seer writes, or causes to be recorded, the revelation upon the principle of plural marriage, in which revelation the sealing power is again restored. A power of the Holy Priesthood which binds on earth and in the heavens. The fullness of this great revelation, with its blessings, powers and privileges, was first given to the prophet Joseph in 1832 A. D.*
In the 10th year, 1844 A. D., we are called to record the culminating events which are still fresh in the memory of Saint and Sinner.

The assassination of the Prophet Joseph Smith, martyred for the cause of truth and the glory of God for the blood thus spilled, was in the fulfillment of prophecy, and the dark, prophetic link of the chain of 45 years, even the 10th link or year, causes the reflections of the writer to pass over a multiplicity of events and to drop a silent tear, refreshed, however, by the knowledge that the time draweth near when he who was thus so foully murdered will, in his glorious resurrected body, again be in the midst of the Saints of God. *Requiescat in passa.*†

Our next consideration will be the 11th link or year in the 45 links or years of Daniel's 1335 years.

*For additional information on the plural marriage relationship, see note at end of this volume. The marriage of Jesus Christ.
† Rest in peace.

The 1290 years of Daniel having already been treated upon are so many years, or links, of the 1335 years, and ended as has been stated in 1834 A. D.*

In treating upon these last years of the 1335, we properly number the links or years from the commencement of the prophetic chain on the going of the church into the wilderness, and the reign of the dark, Satanic power under the name of an apostate Christian church, therefore, in the further consideration of the remaining 1335, is A. D. time, being 1845, corresponds with the 11th link, which is the 1300th link or year of the prophetic 1335 years of Daniel. This 11th link, or year, commences the chain of presidency of Brigham Young and the Twelve Apostles. On the death of Joseph, Brigham Young being president of the Quorum of Twelve Apostles, enters upon his prophetic mission as legal and lawful successor of Joseph Smith, as the presiding authority over the entire church. It having been prophecied many years before by the prophet Joseph Smith, that Brigham Young would be his successor as leader of the people of God with the 2nd presidency of the Church of Jesus Christ of Latter-days. The remaining years of Daniel's 1335 years are 34, ending in 1879.

"And from the time that the daily sacrifice

---

* In this year, 1834 A. D., great trouble and affliction came upon the saints. Being driven from the central stake and the United Order, or "Order of Enoch" being dissolved at the end of the 1290 years, but blessed is he who waiteth unto the 1335th year, when the covenant is again renewed.

53. Therefore, you are dissolved as an United Order with your brethren, that you are not bound only up to this hour unto them, only on this wise, as I said, by loan as shall be agreed by this order in council, as your circumstances will admit and the voice of the council direct. Doctrine and Covenants, Sec. 104.

shall be taken away, and the abomination that maketh desolate set up, there shall be *a thousand two hundred and ninety days.*"
These end in 1834.

"Blessed is he that waiteth and cometh to the *one thousand three hundred and five and thirty days*," or years.
These end in 1879.

We now, keeping the above events in mind, conclude the 45 years of Daniel's 1335 years.

The prophetic mission of Pres Brigham Young reaches over one of the most important and eventful periods of the entire division of the prophetic chain of years, it being not only in the years of Daniel, but also in the prophetic years of Jeremiah; namely, the 70 years that the gospel was to be preached to the entire Gentile nations through the mercy of God. These 70 years, or the first link, corresponds with the year 1835. This year is also the commencing link of the prophetic chain of the prophet Joseph Smith's 56 years.

"It was the will of God that they should go forth, and prune the vinyard for the last time, for the coming of the Lord which was nigh,— even fifty six years should wind up the scene."
Feb. 14, 1835.

In consideration of this important position of Pres. Young there are some events which are clearly marked out in the predictions of the prophets of both the Bible and Book of Mormon.

We enter the year 1847, it being the 1303 link of Daniel's 1335 years, a link for a year. In this year Jan. 14th, the word and will of the Lord came through Pres. Brigham Young to the Church of Jesus Christ of Latter-day Saints at Winter Quarters where the camp of Israel was gathered amidst the

Lamanites belonging to the Omaha Nation, and situated upon the west bank of the Missouri River, near Council Bluffs. From this place commenced the great prophetic journey of the saints through and into the wilderness that was to resound with the "Song of Gladness" and the prayers of the faithful, amidst the people of the house of Joseph.* This year, 1847, witnessed the landing of the saints, under Pres. Young, in the typical valley of the "Jordan," the valley of Salt Lake, situated in the unexplored regions of the great American Desert, being owned by the Mexican Government. Passing over the events of settling of the saints in the "Valley of the Mountains," their hardships, trials and sufferings, we enter the year 1857.

---

* "The wilderness and the solitary place shall be glad for them; and the desert shall rejoice, and blossom as the rose. It shall blossom abundantly, and rejoice even with joy and singing: the glory of Lebanon shall be given unto it, the excellency of Carmel and Sharon; they shall see the glory of the Lord and the excellency of our God.

"Strengthen ye the weak hands, and confirm the feeble knees, Say to them that are of a fearful heart, Be strong, fear not: behold, your God will come with vengence, even God with a recompence; he will come and save you." Isa. 35.

'Oh give thanks unto the Lord, for he is good: for his mercy endureth forever. Let the redeemed of the Lord say so, whom he hath redeemed from the hand of the enemy; And gathered them out of the lands, from the east and from the north and from the south. They wandered in the wilderness in a solitary way; they found no city to dwell in. Hungry and thirsty, their soul fainted in them. Then they cried unto the Lord in their trouble, and he delivered them out of their distress. And he led them forth by the right way, that they might go to a city of habitation. Oh that men would praise the Lord for his goodness, and for his wonderful works to the children of men! For he satisfieth the longing soul, and filleth the hungry soul with goodness. Such as sit in darkness and in the shadow of death, being bound in affliction and iron; because they rebelled against the words of God, and contemned the counsel of the Most High: therefore he brought down their heart with labor; they fell down, and there was none to help." 107th Psalm.

The 1313th year of Daniel's 1335 years or links, 1857. A. D., the power exercised by the Captain of the hosts of Hell, stired up the enemies of the Saints, and the head of the Government of the United States of America, backed up by the National Congress of the people, marshalled and equiped an extensive army, "*the flower of the American Army,*" the veteran troops who had conquered the Mexican nation and engaged in many battles. These the President of the United States, as the Commander in Chief, sent against the Saints. This army, after considerable trouble, drawbacks and adversities, landed in the valley of Salt Lake in the Spring of 1858, and made their camp some 40 miles south of Salt Lake City, passed a little season; and the dark cloud, which hung over the Saints, was dispelled, and the coming of the army with sounding trumpets and great display was entirely defeated, for God had a hook in their jaws. The wisdom of Pres. Young diplomacied this great army out of the country, and the spoils of the same went to enrich the poor, oppressed and thinly clad saints of God; their hunger was appeased, and the 20 millions of money which the coffers of the United States furnished to pay for their folly and oppression, which was the fore-runner of the bloody scene that was to take place in the ending of the 1st woe, or hour, prophetically marked out for Daniel's period, within the 2300 years.

We now come to the prophetic link or year 1317, of Daniel's 1335, or 1861. In this year the first gun of the Rebellion was fired from the batteries which had been erected on the coast of South Carolina, for the prediction had been made in 1832, that the great and fearful bloody wars which were to sweep over the world was to commence at South

Carolina. On the breaking up of the power of the Democratic Party by the election of Abraham Lincoln, a Republican, to the presidency of the United States, South Carolina seceded from the Union of States; other states soon followed. Major Anderson, commander of Fort Sumpter in Charleston harbor was commanded to surrender, refusing, the war was opened. The first gun being fired by the Confederate Army on the early morn of Friday at 4.30 a. m., April 12, 1861.* In the forepart of this year the 2nd woe or hour begins. These three woes will be considered in their proper place. In this year the Congress of the United States passed the "Anti-Poligamy law," this being the first National attact against the religion of the Latter-day Saints.

We now pass over some important and prophetic events, for the present, and consider the year 1874, being the 1330th link. This year concludes the 40 years intervening between the revoking of the order of Enoch, or the "United Order." See note on page 34 of this work.

---

*REVELATION AND PROPHECY ON WAR.—Verily, thus saith the Lord, concerning the wars that will shortly come to pass, beginning at the rebellion at South Carolina, which will eventually terminate in the death and misery of many souls. The days will come that war will be poured out upon all nations, beginning at that place. For behold the Southern States shall be divided against the Northern States, and the Southern States will call on other nations, even the nation of Great Britain, as it is called, and they shall also call upon other nations, in order to defend themselves against other nations; and thus war shall be poured out upon all nations. And it shall come to pass, after many days, slaves shall rise up against their master, who shall be marshalled and disiplined for war.—*Given through Joseph, the Seer, Dec. 25, 1832.*

This war resulted in the loss of hundreds of thousands of lives, and the national debt reached the enormous sum of $2,750,000,000 Jan. 1, 1866, total at the close $4,000,000,000.

In this year, 1874, the Lord renews the covenant or law of Enoch, and commands that the stakes of Zion be set in order. During this order of arrangement, or the work of putting the stakes in order was nearly completed, Pres. Brigham Young was called to enter Paradise for the purpose of completing his mission, which will be refered to elsewhere. Pres. Young departed this life Aug. 29, 1877, being the 1333rd year or link of Daniel's chain of 1335 links.

We now consider the year 1879, which is one of the most important periods of prophecy. It is the last link of the prophetic chain of Daniel's 1335 years. Blessed is he who waiteth and cometh to the one thousand three hundred thirty and five days or years or links, in the ending thereof. He is indeed blessed who is born among the Latter-day Saints with all the oppertunities of education and advancement in every department of life, especially that of correct theoloy, and blessed is all the world, for the privelage they have of being taught in the ways of the Lord, and for the great and grand experience they will get in beholding the prophesyed events taking place and manifestations of the works of God during their lives.

Our next consideration is the prophetic chain of the prophet Joseph Smith, constituting the 56 years before mentioned, commencing with the year 1835. Having already considered the period in brief from the year 1835, to the close of Daniel's 1335 years, we therefore pass to the 45th link or year, when is the Jewish year of Jubilee; namely, the 50th, dating from the organization of the church in 1830, and it being an eventful period we commence with this year as the third division of prophetic numbers in 1880, which begins our final chain of 17 links or years to the end of the 2300 years.

THIRD DIVISION.

Pres. John Taylor occupying a very close, clear and defined position in the transactions of the ecclesiastical and national departments of the Church and Kingdom of God, it becomes our duty to define his propetic place from the Bible, Book of Mormon and the peculiar work, or developments, which are the fulfillment of prophecy both ancient and modern.

Onr first position, in this matter of successorship, is to show an unbroken chain of prophetic numbers. First to be considered is the 1335 years of Daniel, 1290 of these years ended in 1834, this leaves 45 years of prophetic events already enumerated which were to take place within that period.

Second the death of the 1st and 2nd presidents, and the commencement of the 3rd. Also the ending of the 1st woe and the beginning of the 2nd.

In 1844, the 10th year of these 45, Joseph, the Seer was martyred, June 27th.

In the year 1877, Aug, 29th, Pres. Young died, it being the 43rd year of the 45 of Daniel's 1335 years, leaving yet 2 years for the first successor of Joseph Smith to finish Daniel's 1335 years, which 2 years were filled by the Twelve Apostles.

In the year of Jubelee, in the first link of the remaining 17 links of the chain of 2300 links or years, in 1880, John Taylor, who was president of the Twelve Apostles at the death of Pres. Young, was sustained, by the voice of the people, at the general assembly of the Saints, which took place in the 1st year after the end of Daniel's 1335 years, therefore, our chain is unbroken, and the links of the remaing 2300 years begin with the presidency of John Taylor in 1880.

Our position now requires us to consider the last

end of the entire period of time as given by the Angel Gabriel to Daniel. This period, beginning with the rebuilding of the walls of Jerusalem 400 years B. C., and ends in 1896, or 1807 years after the birth of Savior. Having shown up 2279 years of the 2300 years of Daniel, Pres John Taylor's rule commences with the year 1880, with a chain of 17 years or links of the chain of 2300 years, or in other words the 2300 years of Daniel being divided into periods of three divisions; namely, the 1290, 1335 and 2300. The 1335 years ending in 1879, leaves us a chain of 17 links or years to complete the great prophetic chain of the entire period, and ends the 2300 years in 1896.

Having brought our considerations to the presidency of the 2nd successor of the prophet Joseph Smith, we now enter into the consideration of the period as the time covered by the 56 years of the prophet Joseph Smith.

The 1st link of the 17 years, beginning in 1880, corresponds to the 45th year or link of the 56 years, "which winds up the scene," ending in 1891.

The question arises "what scene?" did the prophet mean. This will appear further on.

During the last month prior to the death of Pres. Brigham Young, John Taylor was sent to complete the organization of the Bear Lake Stake, and a short time before Pres. Young died sent word that he had accomplished the mission, and the stakes of Zion were completely organized. See Deseret News, No. 2084.

Therefore, Pres. Taylor, upon entering his high and holy calling, and important period in which he officiates, begins the prophetic years of the Ancient of days time with the last 17 links of the 2300 years of Daniel's time.

The prophetic proof which cluster around the aged silvered brow of our beloved President Taylor shines out with resplendent luster. The rays of light, which are now reaching out, are illuminating the horizon of our Mountain Home, and will grow brighter and brighter until the whole heavenly hosts shall be reached, and the people are brought to that unity of the faith that Zion will shine and in the bosom of each, that thus receiveth the light, the glory of God will be made manifest, *"for if ye are not one ye are not mine."* Let the earth resound, and holy anthems ascend on high, for when ye see signs in the heavens and upon and in the earth, behold, your redemption draweth nigh, and the saints shall be free. Our Capital, which now is the spoil of the enemies of God and His Christ, shall be deserted. Not a dog to break the stillness of the hour, when the Saints shall again possess and tread its soil.

In the 3rd year of the 17 years or links, President Taylor, by direct revelation,* introduced the principles by which the House of God, or the people, could be set in order, and prepare the way for the redemption of Zion, for the Saints to again possess the land of the new Jerusalem.†

This present relationship and condition of circumstances being surrounded with so much prophecy we quote as follows:

---

* The power and authority of the higher or Melchisedek priesthood, is to hold the keys of all the spiritual blessings of the church—to have the privelage of receiving the misteries of the kingdom of heaven—to commune with the general assembly and church of the first born, and to enjoy the communion and presence of God the Father, and Jesus the Mediator of the new covenant. D. & C. Sec. 107.

† The redemption of Zion was shown to the prophet Joseph Smith in vision, as also others, by visions and dreams have seen the glory of Zion, the city of the new Jerusalem.

"So shall they fear the name of the Lord from the west, and his glory from the rising of the sun. When the enemy shall come in like a flood, the Spirit of the Lord shall lift up a standard against him. And the Redeemer shall come to Zion, and unto them that turn from transgression in Jacob, saith the Lord. As for me, this is my covenant with them, saith the Lord; My Spirit that is upon thee, and my words which I have put in thy mouth, shall not depart out of thy mouth, nor out of the mouth of thy seed, nor out of thy seed's seed, saith the Lord, from henceforth and for ever." Isa. 59.

"The sons also of them that afflicted thee shall come bending unto thee; and all they that despised thee shall bow themselves down at the soles of thy feet; and they shall call thee, The city of the Lord, The Zion of the Holy One of Israel." Isa. 60

Many other quotations could be given, but the consideration is the present position and developments of the times, and as we progress to the end of the 17 years or links, which end in 1896, it must be remembered, that we are classifying these prophetic periods under three heads; 1st prophecy fulfilled, 2nd prophecy being fulfilled and 3rd prophecy yet future.

The Book of Mormon has given us a true and perfect system of information, surrounded by a most perfect wall of historical defence, locating the presidency of Pres. Taylor in a prophetic period especially refered to by the Savior when He visited the Nephites some months after His resurrection. The sign and covenant refered to are important considerations, for when properly understood there is no cause for doubt.

When Nephi, in vision, beheld the Gentiles cross the great waters and spread over the promised land,

America, and that they had with them a certain book which they esteemed highly, the angel thus gives information concerning the same:

"And the angel said unto me, knowest thou the meaning of the book? And I said unto him, I know not. And he said, behold it proceedeth out of the mouth of a Jew: and I Nephi, beheld it; and he said unto me, the book that thou beheldest is a record of the Jews, which contains the covenants of the Lord which he had made unto the house of Israel; and it also containeth many of the propecies of the holy prophets; and it is a record like unto the engravings which are upon the plates of brass, save there are not so many; nevertheless, they contain the covenants of the Lord, which he hath made unto the house of Israel; wherefore, they are of great worth unto the Gentiles. . . . .

And it came to pass that the angel of the Lord spake unto me, saying, behold, thus saith the Lamb of God, after I have visited the remnant of the house of Israel, and this remnant of whom I speak, is the seed of thy father; wherefore, after I have visited them in judgement, and smitten them by the hand of the Gentiles; and after the Gentiles do stumble exceedingly, because of the most plain and precious parts of the gospel of the Lamb, which have been kept back by that abominable church, which is the mother of harlots, saith the Lamb; I will be merciful unto the Gentiles in that day, insomuch that I will bring forth unto them in mine own power, much of my gospel, which shall be plain and precious, saith the Lamb; for behold, saith the Lamb, I will manifest myself unto thy seed, that they shall write many things which I shall minister unto them, which shall be plain and precious; and after thy seed shall be destroyed, and dwindle in unbelief, and also the seed of thy brethern; behold these things shall be hid up, to come forth unto the Gentiles, by the gift and power of the Lamb; and in them shall be written my gospel, saith the Lamb, and my rock and my salvation; blessed are they who shall seek to bring forth my Zion at that day, for they shall have the gift and the power of the Holy Ghost: and if they endure unto the end, they shall be lifted up at the last day, and shall be saved in the everlasting kingdom of the Lamb; and whoso shall publish peace, yea, tidings of great joy, how beautiful upon the mountains shall they be. . . . .

And it came to pass that I beheld the remnant of the seed of my brethren, and also the book of the Lamb of God, which had proceeded forth from the mouth of the Jew, that it came forth from the Gentiles, unto the remnant of the seed of my brethren, and after it had come forth unto them, I beheld other books, which came forth by the power of the Lamb, from the Gentiles unto them, unto the convincing of the Gentiles, and the ramnant of the seed of my brethren, and also the Jews, who were scattered upon all the face of the earth, that the records of the prophets and of the twelve aposteles of the Lamd are true. I. Nephi 13.

Other quotations could be multiplied upon the point being considered, We pass to the fulfillment of prophecy concerning the first book called the Bible, which was the book seen by Nephi, and refered to by the holy angel. The man refered to, who was influenced by the Spirit of God to cross the waters to the promised land, was Christopher Columbus. Soon after he had opened the way to America, the land of promise, England became the possesser of considerable of the territory. When a typified period of 169 years had passed, beginning with the year 1492, when the vessels of Columbus landed on the islands of the east coast of America, we date the settlement of the promised land by the Gentiles, it being in 1661. From the Gentiles the Bible was to go forth to the Indians, (Lamanites) the remnants of the land. In 1661, the New Testament was first printed in the *Indian dialect*. In 1663, the Old Testament was first printed in America in the dialect of the then "Great Confederacy," called the Five Nations.

Thus we have the Bible printed first in the Indian language after being brought to the promised land by the Gentiles, seen in vision 2087 years before.

We now consider what relationship, as a type, this fulfillment of prophecy has to the going forth of the Book of Mormon to the Indians, or Lamanites, the remnant of the land.

"And the angel spake unto me, saying, these last records which thou hast seen among the Gentiles, shall establish the truth of the first, which are of the twelve apostles of the Lamb, and shall make known the plain and precious things which have been taken away from them; and shall make known to all kindreds, tongues, and people, that the Lamb of God is the Son of the eternal Father, and the Savior of the world; and that all men must come unto him, or they cannot be saved; and they must come according to the words which shall be established by the mouth of the Lamb: and the words of the Lamb shall be made known in the records of thy seed, as well as the record of the twelve apostles of the Lamb; wherefore they shall both be established in one; for there is one God and one Shepherd over all the earth; and the time cometh that he shall manifest himself unto all nations."

The knowledge of this great work was not to escape the Indians, or Lamanites. There are over 10,000,000 of Indians in North and South America who speak the Spanish language; hence, the close relationship that the Bible and Book of Mormon bear to each other is clearly revealed. As the Bible came to them from the Gentiles, so likewise in the language of the Gentiles, will this great work, the Book of Mormon, go unto the remnants of the land. When the Book of Mormon, or the words of the book, go to the Lamanites, printed in the Spanish language, then will commence the great work of the Father with them and other portions of the house of Israel.

This great work taking place in the time of Pres. Taylor, his place in the great prophetic chain, is clearly marked out. The importance of the introduction of the Bible, that was given in vision, to Nephi, to the Gentiles as well as Indians upon the promised land, is carried still farther, in its prophetic fulfillment as will be seen by the following:

The first American edition of the Bible in the English language was printed by Kneeland and Green, at Boston, in 1772, being 109 years after it was printed in the Indian dialect, as has been stated, which was compiled and printed by John Elliot at Cambridge, Mass.

The remarkable clearness with which the vision was fulfilled cannot but be seen and apreciated by the humble seeker after truth. In Sep. 12, 1782, Robert Atkin obtained a public recognition for the edition of the Bible printed by him in Philadelphia. In 1871-2 a memorial was presented to the National Congress, which was courteously acted upon and a resolution was unanimously adopted, recommending this edition to the people.

The portrature of these and other events have been prophetically outlined at different times from 600 B. C. to 420 A. D., many of which should take place in the generation (100 years) after the coming forth of the Book of Mormon, and in this period Gentile and Jew, Lamanite, saint and sinner have a defined place, and our subject becomes the more intensely interesting in the day of our present President, John Taylor, because of the work assigned unto him, for which the prophetic numbers, or periods of time enumerated in the book of Daniel and the 56 years of the prophet Joseph Smith, are especially noted.

The prophetic division of the dispensation upon which Pres. Taylor has entered will soon develope into a high order of intellectual endowment and advancement generally, including manufacture, the arts and sciences and, especially, revelation from the heavens. See Des. News, Sep. 20, 1884.

Our temples which are now being erected, especially the Salt Lake Temple, will be filled with the knowledge of God, His purposes and decrees.

The time has come for the elders of the church to reform in every condition and relationship of life; to surround themselves with those associations and influences which will prepare them as the temples of God in which the Holy Ghost can operate; and each and every one arrive at that unity of the faith which, in thus becoming a chosen people, will be banded together, having one heart and one mind in all things both temporal and spiritual, that God, in thus having such a people, will hear from the heavens and speadily roll on His great work, for it is by and through such a people that the redemption of Zion only can be consumated, and when His people will obey *the law*, then, surely, will the Lord fulfill His word,* and "I will send one mighty and strong." The truth of this can be clearly shown from many places recorded in the Doc. & Cov.

That there may be no mistake about this people, and the redemption of Zion, or Jackson Co., the land upon which the central, Capital of Idumea will be built, a prophetic period has been outlined and confined within the limits of the prophetic numbers herin given, thus saith the Lord:

"For I the Almighty, have laid my hands upon the nations, to scourge them for their wikedness and the plagues shall go forth, and they shall not be taken from the earth until I have completed my work which shall be cut short in righteousness, until all shall know me, who remain, even from the least unto the greatest and shall be filled with the knowledge of the Lord, and shall see eye to eye, and shall lift up their voice, and with the voice together sing this new song, saying—

"The Lord hath brought again Zion:
The Lord hath redeemed his people, Israel,
According to the elleetion of grace,

---

*Verily I say unto you who have assembled yourselves together that you may learn my will concerning the redemption of mine afflicted people. Behold, I say unto you, were it not for the transgressions of my people, speaking concerning the church and not individuals, they might have been redeemed even now; But behold, they have not learned to be obedient to the things which I required at their hands, but are full of all manner of evil, and do not impart of their substance, as becometh Saints, to the poor and afflicted among them, and are not united according to the union required by the law of the celestial kingdom; and Zion cannot be built up unless it is by the principles of the law of the celestial kingdom, otherwise I cannot receive her unto myself; and my people must needs be chastened until they learn obedience, if it must needs be, by the things which they suffer. I speak not concerning those who are appointed to lead my people, who are the first elders of my church, for they are not all under this condemnation. Doc. & Cov. Sec. 105.

Which was brought to pass by the faith
And covenant of their fathers.
  The Lord has redeemed his people,
And Saten is bound and time is no longer:
The Lord hath gathered all things in one:
The Lord hath brought down Zion from above.
The Lord hath brought up Zion from beneath.
  The earth hath travailed and brought forth her strength:
And truth is established in her bowels:
And the heavens have smiled upon her:
And she is clothed with the glory of her God:
For he stands in the midst of his people:
  Glory, and honor, and power, and might,
Be ascribed to our God; for he is full of mercy,
Justice, grace and truth, and peace,
For ever and ever, Amen. Doc. & Cov. Sec. 84, and Isaiah 52.

The hosts of hell are organizing their forces. The entire machinery of the United States, in church and state, are rapidly being brought to the front, directed by the Evil One, the enemy of Christ, to frustrate the purpose of God.

Our President, the servant of God, who stands at the head of the church, bowed down with age, needs every principle of an endowed union of the people of God. The Almighty will strengthen and give wisdom to our venerable leader, and the power of Saten will be frustrated. This is no common war. It is the captain of the hosts of hell, with his millions of followers, contending against the captain of the hosts of heaven, for the supremacy. The silent onward march of the army of the Lord arrouses the most intense hatred of the opposite power.

Every movement made by Pres. Taylor demonstrates the shortness of the time. The enemy must be fought at every point; every foot of soil must be conquered. The little stone which is cut out of the mountain without hands, striking the image upon the feet, must continue to roll till the kingdoms of this world becomes the kingdom of our Lord and his Christ.*

That sword which had laid in its sheath for 14 centuries, and which now lies unsheathed, has upon its ancient and untarnished blade, this writing:

"*This sword shall no more be sheathed until the kingdoms of this world becomes the kingdom of our God and his Christ.*" See Des. News, August 28th 1877.

Before concluding the prophetic surroundings of Pres. Taylor, we will consider the period of time passed over under the head of the 1st and 2nd woes. These woes, or hours, are periods of years, constituting 41 years and 8 months each.

The 1st woe or hour commenced in 1820, for this reason, that as they are 3 in number each being 41 years and 8 months long and ending in 1945. they necessarily take their places in 1820, 1862 and 1904. The beginning of the 1st woe corresponds to the year when the Father and Son appeared to Joseph Smith in the early Spring of 1820. The fearful scenes which have taken place during this 1st woe are fresh in the memory of each individual.

The 2nd woe or hour is now before us 22 years of which have passed, and how fearful has been the time, but, ere the remainder of this woe is passed, blood like rivers will flow.

The completion of the 2nd woe also completes

---

*The Prophet Joseph, reflecting upon intemperance, said: "Methinks, the earth will be swept with the wrath of God and Christs Kingdom will become universal, ere this monster becomes subdued. O come, Lord Jesus, and cut short thy work in righteousness."

the 70 years of Jeremiah, when the long suffering mercy of God will be brought to a close, and the Gentiles shall "fall to rise no more," for thus saith the Lord:

"Therefore thou shalt say unto them, thus saith the Lord of Hosts, the God of Israel: drink ye and be drunken, and spew, and fall and rise no more; because of the sword which I will send among you." Jer. 25: 27.

The consideration of the remainder of the 2nd woe and the 3rd woe we leave for the present, and the remainder of the prophet Joseph Smith's 56 years will be considered.

Having shown the period in which we now live to be the 17 links, or years which brings in the preparatory work of the Ancient of Days' period, we enter the year 1887.

From the remarkable coincidental fulfillment of prophecy, in the events which are denominated by different degrees of reckoning, our consideration of this year requires some explanation as to the meaning to be applied, and the interpretation of the language of the angel that stood upon the sea and land seen by Daniel, and the angel that stood upon the waters, seen by John the revelator.

Daniel's period is 1260 common days, or time, times and a half; John's period is 1260 days, or years, angel's reckoning of time, also time, times and a half. Daniel's time is 3½ of our years; John refers to our years as day periods of time, thus: when the church, or woman, went into the wilderness in 570, she, having a place prepared by the Lord, was to be fed 1260 periods of time, years. Daniel refers to a period after the church was again organized and afterwards scattered for 3½ years, or 1260 common days, and is considered as follows:

The period that the Church of Latter-days is to conform to, is not a period of synonymous reckoning as relates to time, but a type only. In one case the church rested in a place prepared and was fed; while in the other she was to be nourished for a period of $3\frac{1}{2}$ years, time, times and a half, after being scattered. This period, therefore is before the close of the year 1891, and commences when the star of Bethlehem, will arise in 1887. This corresponds with the prophetic reckoning. Much could be advanced to surround this $3\frac{1}{2}$ years from 1887 to 1891, with prophetic import.

Daniel's Angel thus addressed him, or thus spoke:

"And I [Daniel] heard the man clothed in linen, which was upon the waters of the rivers, when he held up his right hand and his left hand unto heaven, and sware by him that liveth for ever, that it shall be for a time, times and a half, and when he [Michael] shall have accomplished to scatter the power of the holy people, all these things shall be finished."

The power of the holy people being scattered is to be understood as refering to the influence, or government of the priesthood which will continue to grow and increase during these 17 years of the Ancient of Days' time.

It must be understood, in this connection, that Michael has power to scatter the power of the holy people and to gather them again, and will do it in this case. The object of his scattering them is to bring salvation, by the Zion of God among all nations. We have not room here to go into the details of this subject, but it will follow this work soon, and also be given with illustrated lectures in our halls. Please see Doc. & Cov. Secs. 14, 85, 97, and 132 par. 20, Deu. 17; 3, 4; 9,

"Questions by Elias Higbee, as follows—'What is meant by the command in Isaiah, 52nd chapter, 1st verse, which saith,, put on thy strength O Zion? And what people had Isaiah reference to?'

"He had reference to those whom God should call in the last days, who should hold the power of the Priesthood to bring again Zion, and the redemption of Israel; and to put on her strength is to put on the authority of the Priesthood, which she (Zion) has a right to by lineage; also to return to that power which she had lost.

'What are we to understand by Zion's loosing herself from the bands of her neck, 2nd verse?'

"We are to understand that the scattered remnants are exhorted to return to the Lord from whence they have fallen, which if they do, the promise of the Lord is that he will speak to them, or give them revelation. See the 6th, 7th and 8th verses. The bands of her neck are the curses of God upon her, or the remnants of Israel in their scattered condition among the Gentiles." Doc. & Cov. Sec. 113. See also III. Nephi 7.

After this period of 3½ years, when the power of the holy priesthood and government of God has extended, we enter into the time which finds the Capital, or Jackson Co.,* in the hands of the Saints,

---

*"Blow ye the trumpet in Zion, and sound an alarm in my holy mountain: let all the inhabitants of the land tremble: for the day of the Lord cometh, for it is nigh at hand; and the Lord shall utter his voice before his army: for he is strong that executeth his word: for the day of the Lord is great and very terrible, and who can abide it? put ye in the sickle, for the harvest is ripe: come, get you down; for the press is full, the fats overflow; for their wickedness is great. Multitudes, multitudes in the valley of decision: for the day of the Lord is near in the valley of decision. The sun and the moon shall be darkened, and the stars shall withdraw their shining. The Lord also shall roar out of Zion, and utter his voice from Jerusalem; and the heavens and the earth shall shake: but the Lord

the united and pure people who are of one heart and mind and who keep perfect the law of God; this is the time so, often spoken of in the past discources of President Taylor, when he has quoted the prophet Jeremiah 3; 15, . "And I will give you pastors according to mine heart which shall feed you with knowledge and understanding."

Our subject now enters the most important period of time ever the earth has witnessed, and in treating upon events predicted as yet to be fulfilled, we will need another volume, which will follow this as Volume II.

will be the hope of his people, and the strenght of the children of Israel. So shall ye know that I am the Lord your God dwelling in Zion, my holy mountain: then shall Jerusalem be holy, and there shall no stranger pass through her any more. Joel 2; 1, 3; 11-17.

For, behold, the day cometh, that shall burn as an oven; and all the proud, yea, and all that do wickedly, shall be stubble: and the day that cometh shall burn them up, saith the Lord of the hosts, that it shall leave them neither root nor branch. But unto you that fear my name shall the Sun of righteousness arise with healing in his wings; and ye shall go forth, and grow up as calves of the stall. And ye shall tread down the wicked; for they shall be ashes under the soles of your feet in the day that I shall do this, saith the Lord of hosts.

"Remember ye the law of Moses my servant, which I commanded unto him in Horeb for all Israel, with the statutes and judgments. Behold, I will send you Elijah the prophet before the coming of the great and dreadful day of the Lord: and he shall turn the heart of the fathers to the children, and the heart of the children to their fathers, lest I come and smite the earth with a curse." Mal. 4.

Elijah having come, and the word of the Lord having been delivered, the gospel being preached again unto all nations for a half a generation and more, the time is short and the end is nigh, for the Saints shall rule, Zion be free and the glory of God be made manifest! The circle is being enlarged, and the borders of Zion are being extended. Arise ye people of God and prepare yourselves, for surely the calamities which the 2nd woe will bring upon the earth will cause the heart to sicken because of the awful destruction upon the world.

We here make a few extracts from a discourse delivered on Sunday afternoon, Oct. 7, 1883, relating to the destiny of the "Mormons:"

" 'If the world hate you, ye know that it hated me before it hated you.' In other words the Savior said, 'If they love me they will love you; if they receive me they will receive you; if they reject me they will reject you; if they persecute me they will persecute you.' And He further said—and it is singular that He should have to say it to His deciples, men who were good, virtuous, pure, upright and desirous to promote the welfare of humanity—it is singular that He should have to say; 'Blessed are ye when men shall revile you, and persecute you, and shall say all manner of evil against you falsely, for my sake. Rejoice and be exceeding glad; for great is your reward in heaven; for so persecuted they the Prophets which were before you.' Were these men the enemies of mankind because they told them the truth? All intelligent men would say No. Are those Elders who go forth to proclaim the Gospel to-day the enemies of mankind? All intelligent men will say No. Well, would you try to coerce men? No. Why? Because God does not do it, and He does not want us to do it. I would not use any influence but that of truth to lead any man to a knowledge of the truth. Any other influence, any other power, any other spirit is not of God. There is a species of false Christianity that think it is right to presecute People because of their religion, but those possessed of that spirit, whoever they are, are of their father the devil, because his works they do. God believes in the freedom of mankind, and Satan was cast out of heaven because he sought to take away the free agency of man. In various ages of the world, under various guises, the same thing has been attempted. Sometimes political, sometimes religious and sometimes other pretexts are introduced to oppress mankind and to deprive them of that liberty, which is their birth-right, and which all men have a right, under God's laws, to enjoy.

"Now I come to talk of our relationship to this nation, in a political point of view. We are here in this Territory of Utah. We were told to gather here by the Lord and we have obeyed his command, just as they did in the Zion of Enoch in his day. When we came here we brought our bodies with us. It is not a spiritual thing, for we are all of us very literal and very temporal. We have legs and arms, eyes and ears, like other people—we are the children of our Heavenly Father as others are.

"We consider as Latter-day Saints that we have rights here, and although we have been dealt with, as we would call it, rather scurvely by the government that ought to foster us, yet at the same time we have strictly adhered to the letter of the law, even in the face of the assumed purity those people (our enemies) profess to attach to themselves. We have not resisted any of these things, but have treated those men, who came as our oppressors, if you please, with kindness and due respect notwithstanding they have introduced many things in our midst at variance with the laws and Constitution of the United States, and with our rights as American Citizens. We have been treated like a step-child by our Parent Government. Loyal as we are to the core; believing as we do that the Constitution of our Country is inspired of God. We have maintained good order in these mountains, not because governors have been sent here not of our choosing; not because federal officials have been sent here in whose selection we have had no voice; but because there has been a union in the people. God has developed true statesmanship in the midst of these Latter-day Saints. There are hundreds of men in this community who can take a body of people and go into these desert wilds and build up a city, or a number of cities, and govern and control them in a manner that if the whole world were governed in that way would produce the grandest results. We have demonstrated our capacity for self-government and it is inherent in the people, springing from the wisdom and blessing that God has bestowed upon men. There is no community to-day within the confines of these United States that can furnish so many practical men of this character as can the Latter-day Saints, and the evidences of it are to be seen in the good order that prevails throughout these mountains wherever the Latter-day Saints live and have influence.''

CHAPTER III.

THE MARRIAGE RELATION OF JESUS A PLURALITY.

The Bridegroom—Lord and Master—Plural marriage descent—Sealing—Marriage of the Father—Unity brought together in one, etc.

INCIDENTAL to the passage of the Anti-poligamy Bill of 1862, as also the Poland and Edmund's Bills, we here consider the question; was Jesus Christ the husband of one or more wives?* and did He have by them one or more children?†

Our answer is decidedly yes. Our Lord, Jesus Christ was married according to the Jewish custom and form of marriage, and that too at their annual feast called the "Marriage Feast," which took place at certain specified times. These feasts were presided over by a governer. The cerimony and form of the marriage was followed by Jesus in this respect, for the reason of the position of his parents being poor, or in other words Joseph his adopted father, or reputed father, was poor and of obscure origin by reason of the usurpation of the throne of David and the servitude of the Jewish race under the power and rule of the Roman, or 4th diverse beast.

---

* Actual and typified refferences which are consistent with the marriage relationship of our Lord Jesus Christ.— Matt. 22, Luke 22; 28, Rev. 19: 7. and Ps. 45. Many other passages could be added.

† Isaiah 53; 10, Ps. 45; 16.

This marriage of Jesus took place at the marriage feast held in Cana, and the extreme poverty, or circumstances of his parents and himself, found him at this feast without the usual complements of wine.

When, in accordance with the list of names, it came the turn of Jesus, who was named last upon the list, to present himself before the governor of the feast, the servants who officiated at the feast repaired to his mother for the purpose of presenting his gift of wine, etc., for the custom was a Jewish one. She addressed her son Jesus, and informed him that there was no wine.

Jesus, being thus addressed, was made aware of the fact that his hour had arrived, and seemed to understand what was required of him. Now at this feast there were several large vessels of earthenware, which were at the time empty, and the mother of Jesus commanded that the servants should do as her son directed*

Jesus saith unto the servants, "fill the water pots with water," and they filled them to the brim. Jesus then commanded them to draw out and bare

---

*The true translation of the reply which Jesus made to his mother, is as follows: "And on the third day of the week there was a marriage in Cana of Galilee; and the mother of Jesus was there. And Jesus was called, and his desciples, to the marriage. And when they wanted wine his mother said unto him: They have no wine. Jesus said unto her, Woman what wilt thou have me do for thee? that will I do; for mine hour is not yet come. His mother said unto the servants, Whatsoever he saith unto you, see that ye do it."

"King James Bible reads as follows: And the third day there was a marriage in Cana of Galilee; and the mother of Jesus was there; and both Jesus was called and his deciples to the marrige. And when they wanted wine, the mother of Jesus saith unto him; They have no wine. Jesus saith unto her, Woman, what have I to do with thee? mine hour is not yet come. his mother saith unto the servants, Whatsoever he saith unto you, do it." John 2: 1-5.

the same to the governor of the feast, which they did. The superior quality of this wine, made from the water which Jesus had the servants fill the vessels with, caused the governor of the feast to make special refference to it, and in doing so he called the bridegroom and thus addressed him:

"When the ruler of the feast had tasted the water that was made wine, and knew not whence it was, (but the servants which drew the water knew,) the governor of the feast called the bridegroom, and saith unto him, Every man at the beginning doth set forth good wine; and when men have well drunk, then that which is worse: but thou hast kept the good wine until now. This beginning of miracles did Jesus in Cana of Galilee, and manifested forth his glory; and his deciples believed on him." John 2nd chapter.

A plainer translation of this chapter could be given, but the query is who did the governor address as the bridegroom? The rendering of the text as it stands confirms Jesus as the bridegroom. This was the first miracle that Jesus performed, and the marriage made him free and the head of a house; hence he went to do his work and perform his mission and prove the fulfillment of the prophets. The home of Martha and Mary, the sisters of Lazarus, is surrounded with such peculiar associations and relationships that the honest, unbiased mind coucludes at once, especially when the hebrew for Lord, Master, and Husband is consulted, that both of the sisters of Lazarus were the wives of Jesus, "for Jesus loved these sistesrs and their brother.

We have a striking family relationship in Luke, when the Savior comes into Bethany, the village of his own home we may say, where Martha and Mary lived together. Martha took the greater interest in the housework. We are inclined to think that Mary was dilligent, and ordinarily assisted her sister and did her full share of the housework. But some one told her the Master was coming, and in her zeal and love for him she forgot the housework and preparations for supper, and with the rest of the people of the village gathered about him. Both sisters were human like ourselves; but while Mary was intent on the Master's words, Martha was anxious about the supper. Luke explains it "But Martha was cumbered about much serving." So intent was she with this thought in her mind that she comes to the Savior and complains, saying, "Lord, dost thou not care that my sister hath left me to serve alone? Bid her, therefore that she help me." Why would she ask the Savior to bid her sister help her unless he was their husband? She would not thought of such a thing. In this case he commended Mary, and at the same time he kindly and lovingly gave Martha a few words of caution. He repeats her name twice in loving rebuke: "Martha, Martha, thou art careful and troubled about many things: but one thing is needful: and Mary hath chosen that good part that shall not be taken from her." Luke 10: 39-42.

The strong attachment which Jesus had for these two sisters, and consequently for their brother also, is apparent from the natural feelings manifested by the Savior when they addressed him concerning the matter of Lazarus, as it showed his position and the claim they had upon him. "Now Jesus loved Martha and her sister, and Lazarus." John 11: 5. And both of them said; "Lord, if thou hadst been here, my brother had not died." John 11: 21, 32.

When the Roman centurion offered Jesus the vinegar upon hissup there knelt close by, a woman with a sucking babe—"for when thou shalt offer him an offering for sin, he shall see his seed," "who shall declair his generation seeing he is cut off." The blood of Christ is in the church to-day and in due time will be revealed.

Judah being made the kingly line of descent in David, through whom, both by kingly and priestly descent, Jesus Christ sprang; on the kingly line through Solomon to his father Joseph, and in the priesthood line as well through Nathan the son of David to his mother.

To go further back we might trace the priesthood lineage to God, and show it to be almost entirely by plural marriage descent, especially so from Abraham. As Jesus upbraided the Jews for not doing the works of their father Abraham, he sertainly must have done them himself.

The strict conformity to the law by the Savior is clearly shown. David considering the plural marriage of Jesus, says in Psalm 45: 10: "Hearken, O daughter, and consider and incline thine ear, forget also thine own people, and thy father's house; so shall the King greatly desire thy beauty: for he is thy Lord; and worship thou him." Mary Magdalena and Mary were the first to behold the resurrected Jesus, and they fell at his feet and worshiped him.

The Book of Mormon clearly substanciates the plural relationship; and, as he gave the law to Moses, and said unto David, "if thou hadst asked of me, I would have given the more," he could not have rejected or condemned the practice even in the Nephite Nation. For some time after the Nephites had become a great nation and the kingly power ended and a free and independent order of government was established, they kept the law of moses strictly. They had prophets among them who stood to them as the prophets stood to David, Solomon and other kings of Judah and Israel.

In the 9th year of the reign of the Judges over the Nephites, Alma resigned the position of Chief Judge, and, by the voice of the people, one of the Elders of the church, a wise man, selected by the High Priest and Prophet, Alma, was appointed to fill the office of Chief Judge, being the 2nd head officer in the church, under the form of government which had been established by the last king of the Nephites (Mosiah) by revelation. Alma, being the high priest under the Melchesedek order, began to visit the people and teach them in the ways of truth and the observance of the laws of God. On entering into the city of Amoniah the second time, by the direction of a holy angel, he was informed of the person that should entertain him. The man who was to entertain him was also visited by a holy angel and informed of the fact that a prophet of God would be his guest. After having entertained and given rest to Alma and before starting out upon a preaching tour, Amulek (this being his name) had the high priest, Alma, bless him and his house. In confirming the holy and righteous position of Alma before the people of the city where he resided he uses the following language:

"And it came to pass I obeyed the voice of the angel, and returned towards my house. And as I was going thither, I found the man whom the angel said unto me, thou shalt receive into thy house; and behold it was this same man who has been speaking unto you concerning the things of God. And the angel said unto me he is a holy man; wherefore I know he is a holy man, because it was said by an angel of God. And again I know that the things whereof he hath testified are true:

for behold I say unto you, that as the Lord liveth even so has he sent his angel to make these things manifest unto me; and this he has done while this Alma has dwelt at my house: for behold he has blessed my house, he hath blessed me, and my *women*, and my *children*, and my *father* and my kinsfolks; yea, even all my kindred hath he blessed, and the blessing of the Lord has rested upon us according to the words which he spake." B. of M. Alma 10.

We are informed that Alma, after having delivered instruction to his sons Heleman, Shiblon and Coriantor and blessing them, departed and was heard of no more.

"And now, when Alma had said these words, he blessed the church, yea, all those who should stand fast in the faith, from that time henceforth; and when Alma had done this, he departed out of the land of Zarahemla, as if to go into the land of Melek. And it came to pass that he was never heard of more; as to his death or burial we know not of. Behold, this we know, that he was a righteous man; and the saying went abroad in the church, that he was taken up by the Spirit, or buried by the hand of the Lord, even as Moses. But behold, the scriptures saith the Lord took Moses unto himself; and we suppose that he has also received Alma in the spirit, unto himself: therefore, for this cause, we know nothing concerning his death and burial."

This was in the 18th year of the reign of the Judges over the people of Nephi.

The important keys which Jesus gave to Peter, confirm clearly that the sealing ordinances were performed by him before his crucifixion, which keys relate to the plural marriage covenant. These same keys or powers were given and confirmed in the presence of holy angels, by the Almighty, to the prophet Nephi, 51 years after Alma departed out of the land of Zarahemla, being in the 69th year of the reign of the Judges and 56 years before the personal appearing of the Lord Jesus Christ to the Nephites in the land Bountiful.

"Behold, thou art Nephi, and I am God. Behold, I declare it unto thee in the presence of mine angels, that ye shall have power over this people, and shall smite the earth with famine, and with pestilence, and destruction, according to the wickedness of this people. Behold, I give unto you power, that whatsoever you seal on earth, shall be sealed in heaven; and whatsoever you loose on earth, shall be loosed in heaven; and thus shall ye have power among this people. And thus, if ye shall say unto this temple, it shall be rent in twain, it shall be done. And if ye shall say unto this mountain, be thou cast down and become smooth, it shall be done. And behold, if ye shall say, that God shall smite this people, it shall come to pass. And now behold, I command you that ye shall go and declare unto this people, that thus saith the Lord God, who is the Almighty, except ye repent ye shall be smitten, even unto destruction." Heleman 10.

The land of promise, America, being preserved for the purposes of God, it being the land upon which Adam first commenced his reign, the Almigty decreed that no nation should inhabit the land but those unto whom the same should be revealed, and that they should serve him who was the God of the land, even Jesus Christ. In the settling of the land of promise by the Gentiles the God of heaven was with them. Time rolled along, the Gentiles became numerous and God saw fit to make them a free and independent nation. He inspired men and they were outspoken for the cause of freedom. Among them was Patrck Henry, who in thrilling words influenced the elements of freedom and liberty into the hearts of the people.

"Give me liberty, or give me death," the words of Patrick Henry, were echoed far and near. The spark that had for some time showed a dim luster, now was kindled to a flame, and the slumbering cause of freedom broke out in open war. "The country and the people must be free!" On the assembling of the Continental Congress, Sep. 5, 1774, dates the birth proper of the nation of America, which was confirmed and ratified, and July 4, 1776, found the child thus born grown to be a man, independent and free.

War was soon declared to be the ultimatum. The noble Washington was indeed the father of his country and the spirit of God was with him. He was even protected in body by the Almighty, for he was designed to fill a certain mission and become the father of his country. When acting as aid-de-camp to Gen. Braddock in 1775, he was singled out by an Indian chief, who fired at him 15 times without touching him. Washington never received a wound in battle. Some 15 years after, the Indian chief, refered to, made a long journey to see Washington, and told him that at the battle of Monongahela, where Braddock was defeated, he had shot at him 15 times, but the Great Spirit was with him. God was with the people our Revolutionary Sires; but alas, how their sons have degenerated!

The time had come to prepare the land and the people for the coming forth of the gospel and the reign of Him whose right it is to rule, King of nations as he is King of saints! Nephi saw it in vision as follows:

"And it came to pass that I looked and beheld many waters; and they divided the gentiles from the seed of my brethren. And it came to pass that the angel said unto me, behold the wrath of God is upon the seed of thy brethren! And I looked and beheld a man among the Gentiles who was separated from the seed of my brethern by the many waters: and I beheld the Spirit of God, that it came down and wrought upon the man; and he went forth upon the many waters, even unto the seed of my brethren, who were in the promised land.

"And it came to pass that I beheld the Spirit of God, that it wrought upon other Gentiles; and they went forth out of captivity, upon the many waters.

"And it came to pass that I beheld many multitudes of the Gentiles upon the land of promise; and I beheld the wrath of God, that it was upon the seed of my brethern; and they were scattered before the Gentiles, and were smitten. And I beheld the Spirit of the Lord, that it was upon the Gentiles; that they did prosper, and obtain the land for their inheritance; and I beheld that they were white, and exceeding fair and beautiful, like unto my people, before they were slain.

"And it came to pass that I Nephi, beheld that the Gentiles who had gone forth out of captivity, did humble themselves before the Lord; and the power of the Lord was with them; and I beheld that their mother Gentiles were gathered together upon the waters, and upon the land also, to battle against them; and I beheld that the power of God was with them, and also that the wrath of God was upon all those that were gathered together against them to battle. And I, Nephi, beheld that the Gentiles that had gone out of captivity, were delivered by the power of God." Nephi 13.

The reign of the Judges upon the promised land, now called America, under a republican form of government, being organized by revelation from God, is typical of the government of the United States. God inspired the framers of this government and caused them to set up a free and independent nation.

During the session of Congress in the prophetic year 1776, Richard Henry Lee of the State of Virginia, moved that, *"the United* (States of America) *Colonies are and ought to be free and independent States."*

A committee was appointed to draw up a "DECLARATION OF INDEPENDENCE."

At 2 o'clock on the 4th of July 1776, their report was adopted. As unto the Nephites the voice of the people was made the law or principle by which they should be governed, so likewise in the national supremacy of the government of the people of the United States; hence, when the voice of the people rejects the truth, or by their voice countenance iniquity and violate or break the laws of the land delegated to them as is found recorded in the Constitution, they become subject to the wrath of the Almighty.

The mercy of God, however, is long-suffering, and as it was with the Nephites, so likewise will it be with the people of the United States of America. God sent them a prophet and gave him the keys of the sealing ordinances, warning them from that time, that if they did not repent they should be destroyed and but a remnant should be left. . They repented not; they killed some of the prophets, stoned and cast out others, and many were imprisoned and others persecuted unto death. The visitation of the wrath of the Almighty overtook them, and when they assasinated and murdered their chief judges and rulers, the voice of the people went to sustain unrighteous rulings and unjust laws. The nation was overthrown, the government broken up and a fearful destruction overtook them, only one left to record their history.

In the reign of the government of the United States of America, God likewise sent them a Prophet to whom he likewise gave the keys that bind on the earth and in the heavens, that loose on the earth and in th heavens. This prophet, born a son of this free and independent nation, was rejected and martyred, the sealing power repudiated, and like the nation of Nephites, have become so steeped in sin and violation of the established laws of the land that their overthrow is inevitable, for the decree has gone forth unrevokable:—

"That nation that sheds the blood of the prophets, or assents thereunto shall be destroyed."

Joseph Smith, the Seer, gave to this nation, by the authority of God, the keys of salvation, and by written revelation the authority of the sealing ordinances became an established law unto the church forever.

"Verily, thus saith the Lord unto you, my servant Joseph, that inasmuch as you have inquired of my hand, to know and understand wherein I, the Lord justified my servants Abraham, Isaac and Jacob; as also Moses, David and Solomon, my servants, as touching the principle and doctrine of their having many wives and concubines: Behold! and lo, I am the Lord thy God, and will answer thee as touching this matter: . . . . . .

And verily I say unto you, that the conditions of this law are these:—All covenants, contracts, bonds, obligations, oaths, vows, performances, connections, associations, or expectations, that are not made, and entered into, and sealed, by the Holy Spirit of promise, of him who is anointed, both as well for time and for all eternity, and that too most holy, by revelation and commandment through the medium of mine anointed, whom I have appointed on the earth to hold this power, (and I have appointed unto my servant Joseph to hold this power in the last days, and there is never but one on the earth at a time, on whom this power and the keys of this Priesthood are conferred,) are of no efficacy, virtue or force, in and after the resurrection from the dead.

. . . Was Abraham, therefore, under condemnation? Verily, I say unto you, *Nay;* for I, the Lord, commanded it. Abraham was commanded to offer his son Isaac; nevertheless, it was written, thou shalt not kill. Abraham, however, did not refuse, and it was accounted unto him for righteousness. Abraham received concubines, and they bare him children, and it was accounted unto him for righteousness, because they were given unto him, and he abode in my law, as Isaac also, and Jacob did none other things than that which they were commanded; and because they did none other things than that which they were commanded, they have entered into their exaltation, according to the promises, and sit upon thrones, and are not angels, but are Gods.

"David also received many wives and concubines, as also Solomon and Moses my servants; as also many others of my servants, from the beginning of creation until this time; and in nothing did they sin, save in those things which they received not of me. David's wives and concubines were given unto him, of me, by the hand of Nathan, my servant, and others of the prophets who had the keys of this power; and in none of these things did he sin against me, save in the case of Uriah and his wife, and, therefore he hath fallen from his exaltation, and received his portion; and he shall not inherit them out of the world; for I gave them to another, saith the Lord.

"I am the Lord thy God, and I gave unto thee, my servant Joseph, an appointment, and restore all things; ask what ye will, and it shall be given unto you according to my word. . . . . . .

For I have conferred upon you the keys and power of the Priesthood, wherein I restore all things, and make known unto you all things in due time.

And verily, verily I say unto you, that whatsoever you seal on earth, shall be sealed in heaven; and whatsoever you bind on earth, in my name, and by my word, saith the Lord, it shall be eternally bound in the heavens; and whosoever sins you remit on earth shall be remitted eternally in the heavens; and whosoever sins you retain on earth, shall be retained in heaven. And again, verily I say, whomsoever you bless, I will bless, and whomsoever you curse, I will curse, saith the Lord; for I, the Lord am thy God.

"And again, verily I say unto you, my servant Joseph, that whatsoever you give on earth, and to whomsoever you give any one on earth, by my word, and according to my law, it shall be visited with blessings, and not cursings, and with my power, saith the Lord, and shall be without condemnation on earth, and in heaven. . . . .

Verily, if a man be called of my Father, as was Aaron, by mine own voice, by the voice of him that sent me: and I have endowed him with the keys of the power of this Priesthood, if he do anything in my name, and according to my law, and by my word, he will not commit sin, and I will justify him.

. . . . And now, as pertaining to this law, verily, verily I say unto you, I will reveal more unto you, hereafter; therefore, let this suffice for the present. Behold, I am Alpha and Omega. Amen."

A remarkable coincidental event, is the giving of this revelation to the Church of Jesus Christ of Latter-days in the same year of the reign of the government of the United States, as it was in the reign of the Judges, to the Nephites; viz., the 69th year.

That these keys, which were given to Peter, to Nephi and to Joseph Smith, were the same is evidenced, not only from the Bible, Book of Mormon and the Revelation just quoted, but also from the information imparted to us by Pres. Geo. Q. Cannon in his remarks during a sermon given in the 12th ward, S. L. City, and published in the Deseret News, in April 1884.

The Zodiacal Signs and Figures are the ledger, journal and day-book of the 12 sons of Jacob. In these we find the history of the past, the facts of the present and the predictions of the future.

With regard to the time place and order of receiving the keys of the spiritual gifts under the aristocratic government of permission to the world, by or through Lucifer, we quote as follows: "Maximillian Hell, professor of astronomy at Vienna in the year 1772, was one of these; and he advised a friend of his, a physician of good education and considerable merit, to try whether he could not cure diseases by the use of the magnet. This physician was Dr. Frederick Anthony Mesmer, whose name has since become so widely known. He was greatly pleased with the idea, and made a large number of experiments which convinced him that he could exercise a singular influence over his patients. So successful was he, that he soon laid claim to the discovery of a great curative agent in the magnet. Prof. Heil was not satisfied with this state of affairs, and contested the discovery with Mesmer. . . . .

A commission of nine of the leading members of the Academy of Medicine at Paris was appointed to investigate the claims of their doctrine. These men were skilled in the nature and cure of diseases, and they were the last men to whom we should look for a favorable report of a new doctrine unless they were convinced of its merit. For five years they continued to investigate, and at the end of that time, in the year 1831, a report was made favorable to all the leading pretensions of animal magnatism. This report may be summarized as follows: 1st. This force is capable of exerting a powerful influence over the human system. 2d. The effects produced do not depend on the imagination of the subject. 3d. Its action is not alike on all. 4th. Somnambulic sleep may be produced in this way. 5th. During this sleep injuries to the flesh, or even laceration of the nerves, do not cause pain. 6th. The sleeper can ordinarily hear no sound but the voice of the magnetizer. 7th. The nerves of touch and smell convey no impression to the brain unless excited by the magnetizer. 8th. Some sleepers can see with their eyes closed, can foretell acurately the time of the access of epileptic fits or time of their cure, and can discover the diseases of persons with whom they are placed in magnetic connection. 9th. Persons suffering from pains, fits, etc., were partially or entirely cured by magnetic treatment."—*How to become a Clairvoyant.*

With regard to receiving the keys of the spiritual gifts by a theocratic government, a Jesus Christ to the earth, we quote as follows: from Doc. & Cov.

"And now, behold, I give unto you, and also unto my servant Joseph, the keys of this gift, which shall bring to light this ministry; and in the mouth of two or three witnesses shall every word be established." Sec. 6: par. 28.

"Therefore, if you will ask of me you shall receive, if you will knock it shall be opened unto you." Sec. 14: par. 5.

"But it is they who do not fear me, neither keep my commandments, but build up churches unto themselves to get gain, yea, and all those that do wickedly and build up the kingdom of the devil; yea, verily, verily, I say unto you, that it is they that I will disturb, and cause to tremble and shake to the centre." Sec. 10: par. 56.

From the foregoing series of reasoning we have endeavored to show, that Jesus Christ our Lord, having given authority to men in reference to bonds, contracts, sealings, etc., especially in relation to plural marriage, must have practiced it Himself.

One of the most profound and consistent forms of reasoning, as to the marriage relation of the Savior, lies in the works of his Father; and to make matters speedily conform to a grand centre, the 144,000 spoken of in the Scriptures is taken into consideration. These 144,000 are Gods; hence, at some time remote were *first-borns*, therefore, without enlarging upon the evidence, they must have had 144,000 mothers for each to be the first born, and as they are the sons of God their 144,000 mothers must have been the wives of God, or to cover the facts, the wives of Him who was the husband of the mother of the child, who was called by the name of Jesus. According to the circumstances by which our Lord Jesus Christ was surrounded, therefore, did he conform to a principle of work which he. having seen the Father do before him, so likewise did he also.

The relationship as a brother, "our Elder Brother," being the "First-born" of this creation as Christs also are first-borns of all creations; hence, his Father must have had many wives, our mothers, therefore are we brethren. Hebrews 2: 12, 16-17; Psalms 22: 21-22.

A volume could be written to confirm and prove that Jesus Christ, not only was a married man, but had more wives than one; that he sprang entirely through a plural family, rules in the Heaven of the heavens as a plural Sovereign and in every relationship existing in eternity and time and the eternities hereafter to come, stands as the husband of a multiplicity of wives, who are the mothers of multitudes of nations of children as numberless as the sands upon the sea shore, or the stars of heaven.

"Thy throne, O God, is for ever and ever: the scepter of thy kingdom is a right scepter. Thou lovest righteousness, and hatest wickedness: therefore God, thy God, hath anointed thee with the oil of gladness above thy fellows. All thy garments smell of myrrh, and aloes, and cassia, out of the ivory palace, whereby they have made thee glad. Kings' daughters were among thy honourable women: upon thy right hand did stand the queen in gold of Ophir. Hearken, O daughter, and consider, and incline thine ear; forget also thine own people, and thy father's house; so shall the king greatly desire thy beauty: for he is thy Lord; and worship thou him. And the daughter of Tyre shall be there with a gift; even the rich among the people shall entreat thy favour. The king's daughter is all glorious within: her clothing is of wrought gold. She shall be brought unto the king in raiment of needle-work: the virgins her companions that follow her shall be brought unto thee, With gladness and rejoicing shall they be brought: they shall enter the king's palace. Instead of thy fathers shall be thy children, whom thou mayest make princes in all the earth. I will make thy name to be remembered in all generations: therefore shall the people praise thee for ever and ever." Psalms 45.

The Queen of Heaven.—"Moreover Jeremiah said unto all the people, and to all the women, Hear the word of the Lord, all Judah that are in the land of Egypt: Thus saith the Lord of host, the God of Israel, saying; Ye and your wives have both spoken with your mouths, and fulfilled with your hand, saying, we will surly perform our vows that we have vowed, to burn incense to the queen of heaven, and to pour out drink offerings unto her: ye will surely accomplish your vowes, and surely perform your vows." Jer. 44.

"And Enoch said unto the Lord, How is it that thou canst weep, seeing thou art holy, and from all eternity to all eternity? And were it possible that man could number the particles of the earth, yea and millions of earths like this, it would not be a beginning to the number of thy creations; and thy curtains are stretched out still; and thou art there, and thy bosom is there; and also thou art just; thou art merciful and kind forever; thou hast taken Zion to thine own bosom, from all thy creations, from all eternity to all eternity; and naught but peace, justice and truth is the habitation of thy throne; and mercy shall go before thy face and have no end; how is it thou canst weep?" P. of G. P.

Many creations have many heavens and therefore many Queens. This is the glory of plural marriage.

of a theocratic government, as monogomy is the foundation of an aristocratic government. It has been the rule of the aristocractic order from the beginning to direspect the character of females and trample on their virtue.

We do not expect praise for these sayings any more than men of ancient days, the Apostles, our Savior and others, but we antisipate doing good. We will close this chapter by quoting again from Pres. Taylor's discourse in the *News* Oct. 27, '83.

"We have embraced the Gospel. We have placed ourselves in another position from that of the world. We have entered into sacred covenants with the Lord, and He expects us to fulfill our covenants, and those who do not fulfill them will be condemned. There are certain rules and regulations that exist in the heavens as well as on the earth. We are told that before we can enter into the Celestial Kingdom of God we shall have to pass by the angels and the Gods, and if the Latter-day Saints aim at a Celestial exaltation they must live and abide by the Celestial law or they will not get it any more than the Gentiles will. Hear it ye Latter-day Saints! God expects you to be pure, virtuous, holy, upright, prayerful, honest, obedient to His law, and not to follow the devices and desires of your own hearts. God has revealed many things to you and He will reveal many more, He expects you to abide His law, and those who do not want to abide it, had better quit to-day, the sooner the better, for God expects us to do His will in all things. I do not care who it is these words may effect; for God is building up a Zion and that Zion means the pure in heart, the honorable, the upright, the virtuous, and those whose sympathies extend to the promotion of the welfare of the human family."

THE SEVEN HEADS OF THE BEAST.

		B. C.			B. C.
1.	Babelians	2218	5.	Macedonians	200
2.	Egyptians	1921	6.	Romans	A. D.
3.	Babylonians	600	7.	Carthagenians or	
4.	Medo-Persians	400		Vandals.*	456.

THE TEN HORNS, TOES OR KINGDOMS.†

		A. D.			A. D.
1.	England	872	6.	Holland	1815
2.	France	987	7.	Italy	1821
3.	Spain	1479	8.	Belgium	1831
4.	Anstro-Hungaria	1528	9.	Portugal	1834
5.	Prussia	1701	10.	Greece	1838

THE TWO LITTLE HORNS,
that were to make war with the Saints.

Blind Horn, Rome. Seeing Horn, United States.

As a theocracy was the first, as given to Noah in the second creation, so it shall be the last; to the coming forth of which we have the following list of those who testify to the fact, that the "Mormons" are the proper people, in the proper place, at the proper time, according to given reckoning: The quotations are where their testimony may be found.

1. Celestial beings testify in mathematical reckoning of telestial time to the 2300 days. Dan. 8: 14. 2 The Archangel Gabriel testifies to the astronomical reckoning of signs. Dan. 9: 25-27. 3. The following prophets by prophetic reckoning: Isaiah, Isa. 1: 27; Jeremiah, Jer. 25: 27; Ezekiel, Eze. 34: 11-25; Jesus Christ, Matt. 24: 15; Paul, Acts 3: 20-21; John, Rev. 12: 6; Joseph Smith, Brigham Young and John Taylor, page 81, 100-106 of this work.

---

* See Mr, Mede, and Isaac Philips.   † Prophetic History.

PROPHETIC NUMBERS:

—OR—

THE RISE, PROGRESS AND FUTURE

DESTINY OF THE "MORMONS."

VOLUME II.

Astronomical signs—Origin of Man—The Beast with seven heads—The Church of Christ—The female architects of the Universe—Signs of the 2,300 days—Seven orders of governments—The blind little horn, U. S.—10 kingdoms and Kingdom of God—Gathering of the Zion of God—Eternal existence—100 years hence—Summary Table.

INSTEAD of giving a separate volume of a great number of pages, it is thought best to condense the matter, (of which however there is ample for many volumes) and make this work complete in itself, giving only key-words to those who are able to comprehend, for whom this work is designed.

The astronomical signs of the seventh dispensation was given on the 22" of Sep. 1823, in the sixth portal or house of Levi, by the clod-hopping boy Joseph Smith in open vision he minutely details the coming events of our own day and generation from the year 1823, to the year 1945.

First.—A Book should come forth containing a record of the fullness of the Gospel of Jesus Christ; that the word of the book should go forth to the Gentiles, the book itself to be reserved from the children of men until a day of righteousness.

Second.—By the means of the words of the book the seed of Israel are to be gathered to the fold of the Redeemer.

Third.—The Holy Priesthood was to be given.

Fourth.—The Gospel was to be preached.

Fifth.—There was to be a baptism of water.

Sixth.—There was to be a baptism of the Holy Ghost by the laying on of hands.

Seventh.—Persecution will rage, they will try to overthrow the Church but the more it is opposed it will increase the faster.

Eighth.—Those who profess to know the truth, but walk in deceit shall tremble and be angry.

Ninth.—Knowledge will increase.

Tenth.—A people shall be sanctified.

Eleventh.—An inheritance shall be given.

Twelfth.—The Glory of God will be there.

Thirteenth.—The ten tribes will be revealed from the north country.

Fourteenth.—And the Redeemer shall come to Zion.—*Remarkable vision* p. 5.

Time forms no part of duration but follows all things that have a beginning, or a creation; that which is eternal cannot be preceeded by a cause; hence, a creation is but a change of state.

The eternal self-existing, self-seeing, self-luminous being cannot become a father or a mother, but by parental law, that is, of and by their own free will which is eventuality, causuality and comparison, but had to become a son or daughter first.

A boundless space is the place where all things exist, the continuation of all things in space without a change is endless duration. Time must follow all things which have a creation or beginning. Time giveth the degree of motion between points. Motion the amount of heat. The amount of heat gives the degree of light, for light is luminous heat. The amount of light or truth will give the degree of knowledge. The knowledge will give the amount of perception, and the order to which the eternal being or man belongs. If he be of the telestial order of light, or stary element; the terrestial, or lunar light; or if he be of the self-luminous that gives the sun its light; these four orders of beings exist co-eternal with each other in space.

God has but two orders of government; the aristocratic or degenerative order of government of brute force by Lucifer; and the regenerative or theocratic order of government of love, a moral force by Jesus Christ. Without the first order of government there would be no use for the second in animal life, mineral life, vegetable life, and the life of soils, metals and waters.

The Beast with seven heads and ten horns is the aristocratic political power of land monopoly. The woman he carries is the theological power. The *first* head of this beast was Nimrod, the founder of an aristocratic or fatherly government of brute force on the ruins of the theocratic or fatherly government of Noah. The *second* head is the Pharaohs. The *third* is the Nebuchadnezzar or Babylonian. The *fourth* is the Medes, and Persians. The *fifth* is the Macedoneans. The *sixth* is the Romans. The *seventh* head is the Carthagenians that plundered Rome and ruled 12 months. Rev. 17: 6-10.

"And I saw the women drunken with the blood of the saints, and with the blood of the martyrs of Jesus: and when I saw her, I wondered with great admiration.

And the angel said unto me, wherefore didst thou marvel? I will tell thee the mystery of the woman, and of the beast that carrieth her, which hath the seven heads and ten horns.

The beast that thou sawest was, and is not: and shall ascend out of the bottomless pit, and go into perdition: and they that dwell on the earth shall wonder, whose names were not written in the book of life from the foundation of the world, when they behold the beast that was, and is not, and yet is.

And here is the mind which hath wisdom, The seven heads are seven mountains, on which the woman sitteth.

And there are seven kings: five are fallen, and one is, and the other is not yet come; and when he cometh, he must continue a short space."

The ten horns are ten kings. The little horn is the government of the United States of America, the Gentile power that is to make war with the saints; by that war he, (the little horn), is to perfect the saints, the Zion of God, the priesthood of God; all belonging to the order of the Ancient of Days, (the oldest man), will receive the kingdom of God, and on the ruins of all aristocratic governments of brute force will establish a theocratic government of truth, love and virtue. Then men will beat there swords into plowshares and their spears into pruning hooks; then man to man shall be a brother and a friend.

We shall now look at the astronomical signs of our Prophetic Numbers. When God sent the angel from the courts of Glory to instruct Daniel, the *first* sign he gave him was the going forth of a certain decree; the *second* sign was the death of the Messiah; the *third* sign was the destruction of Jerusalem; the *fourth* sign was the abomination of desolation, which is a people professing to be what they are not, the greatest of all delusions, a self-deception, in the temple, the pulpit and the press, the three great leavers for good and evil in the first and second abomination; the first abomination in the days of Christ, the second in the latter days in the order of Elijah and in the order of Elias; the *fifth* sign is the church going into the wilderness; the *sixth* sign is the truth coming out of the earth, the words of a book given to the learned, Isa. 26: 11; the *seventh* sign is the blessed period referred to by Daniel in which Michael, the Great Prince, has to perform his part at the end of the seventy weeks of Jeremiah, the beginning of the third woe.

Sir.—I have read your little book, and I am a lover of free thought, free speach and free press I take the liberty of asking you a few questions.

Q.—On page 39 you say; "that the Church of Jesus Christ held its jubilee of 50 years in 1880," showing that the existence of the Church of Jesus Christ is a fact of the present. Please inform me in which of the Counties of Utah, shall I find that people, that are one in all things? for it is the desire of my soul to be numbered with such a people; such a people only can be the people of the Lord Jesus Christ. He has said; "in vain do you call me Lord, Lord, when you do not the things that I command you."

The Bible informs us that the Church of Jesus Christ has no individual property. Acts. 4; 32-37, Matt. 19; 16-22. The Book of Mormon informs us that the Church of Jesus Christ had no individual property. IV Nephi 1; 1-7. The Book of Doc. and Cov. informs us that the Church of Jesus Christ is to have no individual property, Sec. 78 and Sec. 102. Again Pres.

John Taylor, in speaking to the Saints of to-day said; "Unless you keep the Celestial law you cannot go into the Celestial Kingdom any more than a Gentile can. Those Saints of God who do not wish to keep the Celestial law had better quit to-day, the sooner the better." Deseret Evening News, Oct. 27, '83.

President Brigham Young in an address three years before his death, said; "we have taken the last step we can take in the direction we have been traveling, we have been going every man for himself and the Devil for all:" Deseret News.

A.—Dear Sir:—"As I am also a lover of free thought, free discussion and free press, permit me to say to you that the saving power of a Jesus Christ is as extensive as his creative power, in animal, mineral, vegetable, and atmospheric life, also in the life of soils, metals and waters, and as the Telestial spirit, the Terrestial, Celestial and Self-luminous spirits of man become embodied in element according to their own will, they do become a part and parcel in the Church of Jesus Christ in their time, place and order, and as his love extends to each and every generation, the length of one of His generations being 2555 Millions of our years, and as we, that live to-day in this lowest hell, are at the end of the 1000th generation of this creation which is extended into infinitude by a plurality of wifes, births, deaths and resurrections, I cannot logically locate the Church of the Lord Jesus Christ on the point of a fine Cambric needle, for man was not brought into space from an adjoining chamber by a special act of creation from nothing, nor was he created from the nebulæ, moliculæ or animalculæ.

The science of optics show that man is a self-existing being abstract and independent of creation.

The order are *first* the domestic group of organs, *second* the combative, *third* the social, *fourth* the moral, *fifth* the recollective, *sixth* the perceptive, *seventh* the regulative. Theologically these are the seven eyes that see all things, the seven lamps that enlighteneth all things, and the seven spirits that are in and through all things. These seven spiritual senses use in their order, according to their own will the, "so called", five natural senses, namely the eye, ear, nose, mouth etc., to take cognisance of external things when not magnatized or enwrapped in vision. That great man the Apostle Orson Pratt arranges man as follows:

Into how many grand divisions may the angels be divided? They may be divided into four grand divisions as follows:—First, spirits or angels, who have never been incorporated with flesh and bones. Second, spirits or angels embodied in a mortal tabernacle. Third, spirits or angels disembodied, but waiting for the resurrection. And fourth, spirits or angels embodied in an immortal tabernacle.—The four grand divisions of angels may still further be divided into fourteen different classes as follows:

First Grand Division.—1. Angels never embodied, who kept their first estate. 2. Angels never embodied, who rebelled and kept not their first estate.

Second Grand Division.—1. Mortal men who hear and obey the gospel. 2. Mortal men who never heard the gospel. 3. Mortal men who hear the gospel but do not obey it. 4. Mortal men who hear the gospel and obey it, but afterwards fall away and become sons of perdition.

Third Grand Division.— 1. Disembodied spirits in celestial paradise or place of happiness. 2. Disembodied spirits in terrestial paradise or prison. 3. Disembodied spirits in telestial paradise or outer darkness. 4. Disembodied spirits of the sons of perdition, the most degraded of all.

Fourth Grand Division.—1. Resurrection, celestial angels. 2. Resurrection, terrestrial angels. 3. Resurrection, telestial angels. 4. Resurrection, sons of perdition.—All these classes of beings were in their origin the sons and daughters of God—begotten by or unto him before the world was made.

The "first born" of all this numerous family, was Jesus Christ. He is "the first born of every creature."—Col. I. 15. "The beginning of the creation of God." Rev. III. 14. "The bright morning star." Rev. XXII. 16. At what period in eternity our oldest brother was born, we know not. If we were to judge from the analogy of nature, we should suppose that a period equal to many millions of our years, intervened between his birth and the organization of our present globe. If there is any analogy between the present process and laws of the generation of our bodies, and the previous process and laws of the generation of our spirits; that is, if in the former world, it requires nearly or quite the same length of time to organize, develope, and to bring forth the SPIRITUAL EMBRYO, that it requires in the present world to organize, develope and bring forth the tabernacle, then we can form a faint idea of the vast length of time which must have intervened.

As we pass along with this subject, let us make a few mathematical calculations, founded, however, upon suppositions which are of very imperfect data.

Suppose that the whole number of spirits, designed to take tabernacles in this world, were the offspring of the same parents begotten, and born of the same father and mother, at an average rate of one per year. What length of time would it require for the production of so great a family? In order to give a correct solution of this question, it would be necessary to know the precise number of inhabitants, designed for this globe. But on the supposition that the earth stands eight thousand years, with an average population of five hundred millions every fifty years—then the whole population would amount to (80,000,000,000) eighty thousand millions. Hence upon these suppositions 80,000,000,000 of years must have intervened between the birth of the oldest and youngest. Add to the whole amount of the human family, one third-part of the host of heaven who fell, and the sum would be increased to one hundred and twenty millions, which upon the foregoing positions, would be the age of the "first born." But let us extend our calculation still further and take into consideration the inhabitants of the thirty worlds of our "Solar system." Let us suppose them to exist 8000 of our years, and be peopled in proportion to their surfaces in the same ratio of our world. What would be the amount of inhabitants?

The extent of surface upon these thirty worlds is equal to (12,750) twelve thousand seven hundred and fifty times the surface of our globe: hence the whole number of inhabitants would amount to (1,020,000,000,000,000) one thousand and twenty million of millions. If all these spirits or angels were born of the same parents at the average rate of one per year, then upwards of one thousand billions of years must have elapsed between the birth day of the oldest and youngest.

If they were brought into existence at the rate of

one per minute, it would still require the vast period of (1900,000,000) nineteen hundred millions of years. At the rate of one per second, (30,000,000) thirty millions of years."

The Telestial Church of Christ with its Apostles, Prophets, gifts and blessings of the Holy Ghost with temporal ordinances, these have God placed in the telestial church to bring the Telestial Saints to Christ, this being the preparatory Gospel of Christ, has a perfect organization in every county of Utah. It is to be hoped that those who are to become the Terrestrial Saints of Christ are very plentiful in each and every County of Utah; but the test! *the test!* THE TEST! THE INQUISITIONAL TEST! of the horn that has began among the Mormons, the scarlet colored lady who is trying to spread her Cloak over the much married men of Utah, will soon demonstrate all those who have completed their telestial education and are prepared to enter the second class; namely, the Terrestrial, under the Elias, at the sacrifice of all political rights and domestic comforts. It is to be hoped that all the Saints of God in Utah and elsewhere, that have sacrificed their homes and friends again and again for the love of truth, and have been under the care of Apostles and Prophets for many years having the gifts and blessings of the Holy Ghost with many temporal ordinances, will become members of the class of Elijah, that is to become one in all things, that the will of God may be done on earth as it is in heaven.

The time has come for the dragon to be cast from the land of Joseph to the earth, his own place for a time. It is the united effort of the Saints of the most High God in this the last struggle for the capital of Idumea, Jackson Co., Mo., that will get the underhold of the dragon by a system of self-government and the sacrifice of all earthly pleasures. In this matter you have the precept and noble example of Pres. John Taylor, Pres. Geo. Q. Cannon and Pres. Jos. F. Smith before you for a patern.

A revelation to Pres John Taylor, Oct. 13" 1882. "Thus saith the Lord, it is not meat that men, who will not abide my law, shall preside over my priesthood; then proceed forthwith and call to your aid and assistance those you may require from among the seventies to assist you in your labor in introducing and maintaining the Gospel among the Lamanites throughout the land and then let high priests be selected under the direction of the first Presidency over the various organizations that shall exist among this people, that those who receive the Gospel may be taught in the doctrines of the Church and laws thereof, and also in the things pertaining to my Zion and my Kingdom, saith the Lord, that they may be one with you in my Church and my Kingdom. Let the Presidency of my Church be one in all things, and let the Twelve, also, be one in all things, and let them all be one with me, as I am one with the Father."

Q.—On page 42 you say that in 1882 the law was revealed to Pres. John Taylor that was to put the House of God in order, which implies that the House of God was out of order up to that time.

A.—The House of God consists of many orders, and each order is a part of the House, having its own laws, ordinances and priesthood. The fullness of the telestial gospel is for the Gentiles with the gifts and blessings of the Holy Ghost and the ministery of Angels; but they cannot see the face of God nor hear His voice. Book of Mormon, III Nephi 7: 2.

Compendium, page 287. Doc. and Cov., Sec. 7, also Sec. 76.

The Terrestrial Gospel of Jesus Christ, under Elijah, the law or class of oneness has the power of seeing God face to face. This law of oneness was revealed to the Church of Christ in this dispensation, but because of the transgression of some, it was revoked. See note on page 34. In the mercy of God it has been restored to Pres. John Taylor in 1882, that all who wish, may sanctify their hearts, purify their affections and clean their hands, by pulling together, with a long pull, and a strong pull, and a pull altogether. Their is no power on earth, or in hell, that can stop such a pull, from placing a theocratic government, of fatherly love, upon the ruins of all brute force governments, that truth and righteousness may prevail upon the earth.

Doc. and Cov. "Verily thus saith the Lord, it shall come to pass that every soul who forsaketh their sins and cometh unto me, and calleth on my name, and obeyeth my voice, and keepeth my commandments, shall see my face and know that I am, and that I am the true light that lighteth every man that cometh into the world; and that I am in the Father, and the Father in me, and the Father and I are one: the Father because he gave me of his fullness, and Son because I was in the world and made flesh my tabernacle, and dwelt among the sons of men."

"Hearken, O ye people of my church, for verily I say unto you, that these things were spoken unto you for your profit and learning; but notwithstanding those things which are written, it always has been given to the elders of my church from the beginning, and ever shall be, to conduct all meetings as they are directed and guided by the Holy Spirit:

nevertheless ye are commanded never to cast any one out from your puplic meetings, which are held before the world; ye are also commanded not to cast any one, who belongeth to the church, out of your sacrament meetings, nevertheless, if any have tresspassed, let him not pertake until he makes reconciliation.

And, again, I say unto you, ye shall not cast any out of your sacrament meetings, who is earnestly seeking the kingdom: I speak this concerning those who are not of the church.

And, again, I say unto you, concerning your confirmation meetings, that if there be any that is not of the church, that is earnestly seeking after the kingdom, ye shall not cast them out; but ye are commanded in all things to ask of God, who giveth liberally; and that which the spirit testifies unto you, even so I would that ye should do in all holiness of heart, walking uprightly before me considering the end of your salvation, doing all things with prayer and thanksgiving, that ye may not be seduced by evil spirits, or doctrines of devils, or the commandments of men, for some are of men, and others of devils.

Wherefore, beware lest ye are deceived; and that ye may not be deceived, seek ye earnestly the best gifts always remembering for what they are given; for verily I say unto you, they are given for the benefit of those who love me and keep all my commandments, and him that seeketh so to do, that all may be benefited that seeketh or that asketh of me, that asketh and not for a sign that he may consume it upon his lusts."

As the iron shroud of oppression is no better in the hands of a "Mormon" Apostle, than in the hands of a popish priest, or a Protestant clergyman; therefore, the word to Zion is, all of you who have the independency of soul and nobility of character to sacrifice your political rights and domestic happiness, must form a nucleus of truth and virtue, around which nucleus will be gathered all the lovers of truth and virtue from every state and nation. God is using the angels of darkness, belonging to the blind little horn, the United States of America, to prepare you for the City of Refuge. See Isa., 28: 16-26; 20: 21.

Doc. and Cov. "Hearken, O ye elders of my church, and give ear to my word, and learn of me what I will concerning you, and also concerning this land unto which I have sent you: for verily I say unto you, blessed is he that keepeth my commandments, whether in life or death; and he that is faithful in tribulation, the reward of the same is greater in the kingdom of heaven.

Ye can not behold with your natural eyes, for the present time, the design of your God concerning those things which shall come hereafter, and the glory which shall follow after much tribulation. For after much tribulation cometh that ye shall be crowned with much glory; the hour is not yet but is nigh at hand."

"Wherefore I, the Lord, have said, gather ye out from the eastern lands, assemble ye yourselves together ye elders of my church; go ye forth unto the western countries, call upon the inhabitants to repent, build up churches unto me; and with one heart and with one mind, gather up your riches that ye may purchase an inheritance which shall hereafter be appointed unto you, and it shall be called the New Jerusalem, and land of peace, a city of refuge, a place of safety for the Saints of the most high God; and the glory of the Lord shall be there, and the terror of the Lord also shall be there, insomuch that the wicked will not come unto it, and it shall be called Zion.

And it shall come to pass, among the wicked, that every man that will not take his sword against his neighbor, must needs flee unto Zion for safety. And there shall be gathered unto it out of every nation under heaven; and it shall be the only people that shall not be at war one with another And it shall be said among the wicked, let us not go up to battle against Zion, for the inhabitants of Zion are terrible; wherefore we cannot stand."

"And now I give unto you a word concerning Zion. Zion shall be redeemed, although she is chastened for a little season. Therefore let your hearts be comforted, for all things shall work together for good to them that walk uprightly, and to the sanctification of the church; for I will raise up unto myself a pure people, that will serve me in righteousness; and all that call on the name of the Lord and keep His commandments, shall be saved. Even so. Amen."

In the State of Pennsylvania God had a people that obeyed His laws, for He revealed Himself to His flock in April 1829; Doc. and Cov., Sec. 6: 34-37. The Lord, in speaking to His Church in May 1829, said: "Therefore, whosoever belongeth to my church need no fear, for such shall inherit the kingdom of heaven." Sec. 10: 55. In June 1829 the Lord said: "Seek to bring forth and establish my Zion. Keep my commandments in all things..... Behold, I am Jesus Christ the Son of the living God, who created the heavens and the earth; a light which cannot be hid in darkness; *wherefore I MUST bring forth the FULLNESS of my Gospel* from the Gentiles unto the House of Israel."

Sec. 14: 6, 9-10. On the following April the Church was organized by the command of God, 1830. And the same day, month and year was the Church organized by the inspiration of the Holy Ghost. Sec. 21: 2. In June following: "For it is because of your dead works, that I have caused this last covenant and this church to be built up unto me, even as in the days of old." Sec. 22: 3. In the month of March following, the Lord said; "ye are also commanded not to cast any one who belongeth to the church out of your sacrament meeting, nevertheless if any have tresspassed let him not partake unless he make reconciliation." Sec. 46: 1-7. (See note on page 34.)

A people in this generation that have seen the face of God and heard his voice in 1829.

Doc. and Cov. "Verily, verily I say unto you, as I said unto my disciples, where two or three are gathered together in my name, as touching one thing, behold, there will I be in the midst of you. Fear not to do good, my sons, whatsoever ye sow, that shall ye also reap; therefore, if ye sow good, ye shall also reap good for your reward.

Therefore fear not little flock, do good; let earth and hell combine against you, for if ye are built upon my Rock, they cannot prevail. Behold, I do not condemn you, go your ways and sin no more, perform with soberness the work which I have commanded you; look unto me in every thought; doubt not, behold the wounds which pierced my side, and also the prints of the nails in my hands and feet; be faithful, keep my commandments, and ye shall inherit the kingdom of heaven. Amen."

"And they who are not sanctified through the law which I have given unto you; even the law of Christ, must inherit another kingdom, even that of a terrestrial kingdom, or that of a telestial kingdom. For he who is not able to abide the law of a celestial kingdom, cannot abide a celestial glory; and he who cannot abide the law of a terrestrial kingdom, cannot abide a terrestrial glory; he who cannot abide the law of a telestial kingdom, cannot abide a telestial glory: therefore he is not meet for a kingdom of glory. Therefore he must abide a kingdom which is not a kingdom of glory.

And, again, verily I say unto you, the earth abideth the law of a celestial kingdom, for it filleth the measure of its creation, and transgresseth not the law. Wherefore it shall be sanctified; yea, notwithstanding it shall die, it shall be quickened again, and shall abide the power by which it is quickened, and the righteous shall inherit it: for notwithstanding they die, they also shall rise again a spiritual body: they who are of a celestial spirit, shall receive the same body which was a natural body; even ye shall receive your bodies, and your glory shall be that glory by which your bodies are quickened. Ye who are quickened by a portion of the terrestrial glory shall then receive of the same, even a fullness; and also they who are quickened by a portion of the telestial glory, shall then receive of the same, even a fullness; and they who remain shall also be quickened; nevertheless they shall return again to their own place, to enjoy that which they are willing to receive, because they were not willing to enjoy that which they might have received."

"Also, I give unto you a commandment, that ye shall continue in prayer and fasting from this time forth. And I give unto you a commandment, that you shall teach one another the doctrine of the kingdom; teach ye dilligently and my grace shall attend you, that you may be instructed more perfectly in theory, in principle, in doctrine, in the law of the Gospel, in all things that pertain unto the kingdom of God, that is expedient for you to understand; of things both in heaven and in earth, and under the earth; things which have been, things which are, things which must shortly come to pass; things which are at home, things which are abroad; the wars and perplexities of the nations, and the judgments which are upon the land, and a knowledge also of countries and kingdoms, that ye may be prepared in all things when I shall send you again to magnify the calling whereunto I have called you, and the mission with which I have commissioned you."

"Art thou a brother or brethren? I salute you in the name of the Lord Jesus Christ, in token or remembrance of the everlasting covenant, in which covenant I receive you to fellowship, in a determination that is fixed, immoveable, and unchangeable, to be your friend and brother through the grace of God, in the bonds of love, to walk in all the commandments of God blameless, in thanksgiving, for ever and ever. Amen.

And he that is found unworthy of this salutation, shall not have place among you: for ye shall not suffer that mine house shall be polluted by them."

Rev. 3. 14-22. "And unto the angel of the church of the Laodiceans write; These things saith the Amen, the faithful and true witness, the beginning of the creation of God;

I know thy works, that thou art neither cold nor hot: I would thou wert cold or hot.

So because thou art lukewarm, and neither cold nor hot, I will spew thee out of my mouth.

Because thou sayeth, I am rich, and increased

with goods, and have need of nothing; and knowest not that thou art wretched, and miserable, and poor, and blind and naked:

I counsel thee to buy of me gold tried in the fire that thou mayest be rich; and white raiment, that thou mayest be clothed, and that the shame of thy nakedness do not appear; and annoint thine eyes with eyesalve, that thou mayest see.

As many as I love, I rebuke and chasten: be zealous therefore, and repent. Behold, I stand at the door, and knock: if any man hear my voice, and open the door, I will come in to him, and will sup with him, and he with me.

To him that overcometh will I grant to sit with me in my throne, even as I also overcame, and am set down with my Father in his throne.

He that hath an ear, let him hear what the Spirit saith unto the churches."

Doc. and Cov. "The Lord spake unto Enoch saying, Hearken unto me saith the Lord your God, who are ordained unto the high priesthood of my church, who have assembled yourselves together; and listen to the counsel of him who has ordained you from on high, who shall speak in your ears the words of wisdom, that salvation may be unto you in that thing which you have presented before me, saith the Lord God; for verily I say unto you, the time has come, and is now at hand; and behold, and lo, it must needs be that there be an organization of my people, in regulating and establishing the affairs of the storehouse for the poor of my people, both in this place and the land of Zion, or in other words, the city of Enoch, for a permanent and everlasting establishment and order unto my church, to advance the cause, which ye have espoused to the salvation of man, and to the glory of your Father who is in heaven, that you may be equal in the bands of heavenly things; yea, and earthly things also, for the obtaining of heavenly things; for if ye are not equal in earthly things, ye cannot be equal in obtaining heavenly things; for if you will that I give unto you a place in the celestial world, you must prepare yourselves by doing the things which I have commanded you and required of you."

TESTIMONY OF PRESIDENT JOHN TAYLOR.

"The Gospel that has been revealed to us is, as it was in Jesus' time, glad tidings of great joy to all people who will receive it and be governed by it. It has a tendency to bring into subjection the wayward passions of men. It teaches us to control our actions, to be subject to all correct laws and to all correct government, to seek unto the Lord for guidance and direction in all our ways, to fear God individually and collectively in our families, and to treat our neighbors, our friends, our brethren, and all men kindly, and not to seek the injury of any person or any nation, nor to plot or contrive or enter into any machinations or combinations to injure anyone.

The revelations which have been given to us some forty or fifty years ago, and that are recorded in the Book of Doctrine and Covenants, tell us of the very state of things that are in existence to-day in this nation and other nations. They tell us about secret plots and contrivances which should be organized with the view of upsetting governments and destroying men. And the Book of Mormon when reference is made to the age in which we live, it is written (II Nephi, XXVI, 22): "And there are also secret combinations, even as in times of old, according to the combinations of the devil, for he is the foundation of all these things; yea, the foundation of murder, and works of darkness; yea, and he leadeth them by the neck with a flaxen cord, until he bindeth them with his strong cords forever." And in another place, referring to the same era (Mormon VIII, 40), the inquiry is made: "Yea, why do you build up you secret abominations to get gain, and cause that widows should morn before the Lord, and also orphans to mourn before the Lord; and also the blood of their fathers and their husbands to cry unto the Lord from the ground for vengeance upon your heads?" You Latter-day Saints, for it is to you I am speaking here to-day. These plots and combinations are instigated by the powers of darkness, and so are the evils that they are designed to correct, They are all from the same source—oppression, in many instances, on the one hand, and combination and resistance on the other—all without any guidance from above or any direction from the Almighty, each man pursuing his own course and following the devices and desires of his own heart. Confidence is being betrayed, right trampled under foot, and hypocrisy on every hand. Those very men who preach to us about our supposed licenciousness are wallowing in filth, corruption and degradation, and I often say, "My soul, enter not thou into their secrets; mine honor, with them be not thou united."—*Des. News.* May 4th, 1884. See also page 78.

TESTIMONY OF PRESIDENT GEORGE Q. CANON

"There are men who say: Yield this practice for the present; perhaps public opinion may soften and then this principle may be taught and practiced.

I look upon such a suggestion as from the devil. It would be quite as proper to propose apostasy for a short season until puplic opinion would become more favorable to us. If there are any in the Church who cannot stand the pressure, instead of talking compromise, let them withdraw quietly from the Church. If they can see nothing in the principle of celestial marriage worth contending for, leave those who do see and appreciate its value to fight the battle alone. The latter will then neither be weakened nor betrayed by the association of those who, in their hearts, stand ready to yield. If there are men in the Church who love the world and its favor better than they do God and truth, or if they fear man's displeasure and punishment more than they love eternal exaltation, now is a good time for them to exhibit the feeling. But if they have any regard left for those who have been their friends and brethren, they ought not, while professing to be members of the Church, to be consorting with those who are its deadly enemies and assenting to their plans for the destruction of a vital principle of exaltation. They should have so much self-respect that while professing to worship Jehovah, they will not prostrate themselves before the image of Baal."—*Juvenile Instructor.* Vol. 20 No. 10.

TESTIMONY OF PRESIDENT JOSEPH F. SMITH.

"Why, then should we be proscribed? Why, then, should the people of the world malign us and seek to blacken our names and our characters? Why should they seek to bring persecution and evil upon us? The answer is to be found in the words of the Savior. "I have chosen you out of the world, and therefore the world hate you." So long as you maintain the principles of the Gospel; so long as you defend and practice the principles of virtue, of truth and righteousness; so long as you stand by the doctrines of Christ, which have been revealed through Joseph the Prophet, through Brigham Young the Prophet, and through President Taylor and the oracles of God; so long the world will be arrayed against you, so long they will hate you and will seek to bring evil upon you unless they repent; but the work of God cannot fail. It is His work He hath decreed its consumation, and no power on earth or in hell can alter the decree. The work is marching forward, and if we do not keep pace with it we must eventually be left behind. Better far for us to keep up with the rank and file, and to walk shoulder to shoulder with the authorities of the Church; with those who have the spirit of the Gospel in their hearts; with those in whose bones burn the fire of truth and the testimony of Jesus Christ who are continually exhorting the people to be diligent in keeping the commandments of God. We should do what is right. We should be virtuous, honorable and charitable, and we should be liberal in our hearts to all mankind. We can afford to be liberal. We have received that which pertains to eternal growth, to eternal increase to eternal happiness; we have received that which pertains to dominion and power and glory and to thrones and principalities. Freely we have received, and freely we can afford to give; for in giving we do not diminish our own store. We can afford, therefore, to exclaim, (in relation to our enemies) "'Father forgive them, for they know not what they do." We can afford to have sympathy for them, to beseech God in the name of Jesus to have mercy upon them, for they no not the consequences of their acts. It is for us to work righteousness; for as President Young remarked in the Temple at St. George, in 1877, the more righteous we are, the more united we are; the more diligent we are in keeping the commandments of God, the less will be the power of our enemies; their power will diminish in proportion to our faithfullness. Yet our enemies will rage and their anger will increase against the work of the Lord; and I persume it is a true saying that "whom the gods would destroy they first make mad." The heathen—the so-called Christian nations—will become mad with rage against the Latter-day Saints, and thus the world will go on until they are ripened for destruction.— *Discourse* in Paris, Idaho, Aug. 19, 1883.

The articles on faith, Doc. and Cov. Lecture VI. "For a man to lay down his all, his character and reputation, his honur and applause, his good name among men, his houses, lands, his brothers and sisters, his wife and children, and even his life also —counting all things but filth and dross for the excellency of the knowledge of Jesus Christ—requires more than mere belief or supposition that he is doing the will of God; but actual knowledge, realizing that, when these sufferings are ended, he will enter into eternal rest, and be a partaker of the glory of God.

For unless a person does know that he is walking according to the will of God, it would be offering an insult to the dignity of the Creator, were he to say, that he would be a partaker of his glory when he should be done with the things of this life. But when he has this knowledge, and most assuredly knows that he is doing the will of God, his confidence can be equally strong that he will be a partaker of the glory of God.

Let us here observe, that a religion that does not require the sacrifice of all things, never has power sufficient to produce the faith necessary unto life and salvation; for, from the first existence of man the faith necessary unto enjoyment of life and salvation never could be obtained whithout the sacrifice of all earthly things. It was through this sacrifice and this only, that God has ordained that men should enjoy eternal life.

A SINGULAR DOCUMENT.

"It is an extract from a letter received bo Dr. Usha, Lord Primate of Ireland. It is dated March 1, 1639, and came from a learned clergyman of the Church of England:

"I was lately looking for a word, and lighted upon a strange passage, that in the reign of Justinian the Emperor, one Theodosious, a Jew, a man of great authority, lived in Jerusalem, with whom a rich goldsmith, who was a Christian, was much in favor and very familar. The goldsmith, in private discourse, told him one day that he wondered he, being a man of such great understanding, did not turn Christian, considering how he found all the prophecies of the law so evidently accomplished in our Savior, and our Savior's prophecies accomplished since. Theodosious answered that it did not stand with his security and continuance in authority to turn Christian, but had a long time a good opinion of that religion, and he would discover a secret to him which was not come to the knowledge of any Christian. It was that when the temple was founded in Jerusalem there was twenty-two priests, according to the number of the Hebrew letters, to officiate in the temple; and when any was chosen, his name, with his father and mother's, were used to be registered in a fair book. In the time of Christ a priest died and one was chosen in his place; but when his name was to be entered his father, Joseph being dead, his mother was sent for who being asked who was his father? she answered that she never knew a man, but that she was conceived by an angel. So his name was registered in these words: 'Jesus Christ the Son of God and of the Virgin Mary.' This record, at the destruction of the temple, was preserved."

Doc. and Cov. "Hearken, O ye people who profess my name, saith the Lord your God, for, behold, mine anger is kindled against the rebellious and they shall know mine arm and mine indignation in the day of visitation and of wrath upon the nations. And he that will not take up his cross and follow me, and keep my commandments, the same shall not be saved."

"Wo unto you rich men, that will not give your substance to the poor, for your riches will canker your souls; and this shall be your lamentation in the day of visitation, and of judgment, and of indignation—The harvest is past, the summer is ended, and my soul is not saved! Wo unto you poor men, whose hearts are not broken, whose spirits are not contrite, and whose bellies are not satisfied, and whose hands are not stayed from laying hold upon other men's goods, whose eyes are full of greediness, who will not labor with their own hands!

But blessed are the poor who are pure in heart, whose hearts are broken, and spirits are contrite, for they shall see the kingdom of God coming in power and great glory unto their deliverance; for the fatness of the earth shall be theirs. For behold the Lord shall come, and his recompense shall be with him, and he shall reward every man, and the poor shall rejoice; and their generations shall inherit the earth from generation to generation, forever and ever."

"For Zion must increase in beauty and in holiness; her borders must be enlarged; her stakes must be strengthened; yea, verily I say unto you, Zion must arise and put on her beautiful garments; therefore I give unto you this commandment, that ye bind yourselves by this covenant, and it shall be done according to the laws of the Lord. Behold, here is wisdom also in me for your good. And you are to be equal, or in other words, you are to have equal claims on the properties, for the benefit of managing the concerns of your stewardships, every man according to his wants and his needs, inasmuch as his wants are just; and all this for the benefit of the church of the living God, that every man may improve upon his talent, that every man may gain other talents, yea, even an hundred fold, to be cast into the Lord's storehouse, to become the common property of the whole church, every man seeking the interest of his neighbor, and doing all things with an eye single to the glory of God.

This order I have appointed to be an everlasting order unto you and unto your successors, inasmuch as you sin not; and the soul that sins against this covenant and hardeneth his heart against it, shall be dealt with according to the laws of my church, and shall be delivered over to the buffetings of Satan until the day of redemption."

"Verily I say unto you who have assembled yourselves together that you may learn my will concerning the redemption of mine afflicted people.

Behold, I say unto you, were it not for the transgressions of my people, speaking concerning the church and not individuals, they might have been redeemed even now; but behold, they have not learned to be obedient to the things which I require at their hands, but are full of all manner of evil, and do not impart of their substance, as becometh Saints, to the poor and afflicted among them, and are not united according to the union required by the law of the celestial kingdom; and Zion cannot be built up unless it is by the principles of the law of the celestial kingdom, otherwise I cannot receive her unto myself; and my people must needs be chastened until they learn obedience, if it must needs be, by the things which they suffer.

I speak not concerning those who are appointed to lead my people, who are the first elders of my church, for they are not all under this condemnation but I speak concerning my churches abroad—there are many who will say—Where is their God? Behold, he will deliver in time of trouble, otherwise we will not go up unto Zion, and will keep our monies. Therefore, in consequence of the transgression of my people, it is expedient in me that mine elders should wait for a little season for the redemption of Zion, that they themselves may be prepared, and that my people may be taught more perfectly, and have experience, and know more perfectly concerning their duty, and the things which I require at their hands; and this cannot be brought to pass until mine elders are endowed with power from on high; for behold, I have prepared a great endowment a blessing to be poured out upon them, inasmuch as they are faithful and continue in humility before me; therefore it is expedient in me that mine elders should wait for a little season for the redemption of Zion; for behold, I do not require at their hands to fight the battles of Zion; for, as I said in a former commandment, even so will I fulfil. I will fight your battles."

And they understood me not that I said they shall hear my voice; and they understood me not that the Gentiles should not at any time hear my voice; that I should not manifest myself unto them, save it were by the Holy Ghost But behold, ye have both heard my voice, and seen me; and ye are my sheep, and ye are numbered among those whom the Father hath given me."

The salvation of the Gentiles in perfection is embodied in the power of the Holy Ghost and the ministering of Angels, which is the Gospel of Elias, which is the saving power of the Lord Jesus Christ to all men of every size, shape and color, with as many degrees or orders of salvation as there are stars in the telestial heaven. This is the Gospel not that gathers all kinds. Mark 16: 16. From this gathering is chosen those that obey the law of oneness and celestial marriage embodied in the revelation of 1882, for the last time, and woe! woe! to them that reject it. The Zion of God that have been gathered from the Gentiles and are called Gentiles and their children, the daughters of Zion, have a great work to do now, for the redemption of the New Jerusalem, after God has gathered out his believing Saints from the unbelieving Saints that under the protection of the "little horn," shall be regarded as the heathen.

Book of Mormon: "But if the Gentiles will repent, and return unto me, saith the Father, behold they shall be numbered among my people, O house of Isreal; and I will not suffer my people, who are of the house of Israel, to go through among them, and tread them down, saith the Father. But if they will not turn unto me, and hearken unto my voice, I will suffer them yea, I will suffer my people, O house of Isreal, that they shall go through among them, and shall tread them down, and they shall be as salt that hath lost its savor, which is thenceforth good for nothing, but to be cast out and to be trodden under foot of my people, O house of Isreal.

Verily, verily, I say unto you, thus hath the Father commanded me, that I should give unto this people this land for their inheritance. And when the words of the prophet Isaiah shall be fulfilled, which say, thy watchmen shall lift up the voice; with the voice together shall they sing, for they shall see eye to eye, when the Lord shall bring again Zion. Break forth into joy, sing together; ye waste places of Jerusalem, for the Lord hath comforted his people, he hath redeemed Jerusalem. The Lord hath made bare his holy arm in the eyes of all the nations; and all the ends of the earth shall see the salvation of God."

"Yea, wo be unto the Gentiles, except they repent, for it shall come to pass in that day, saith the Father that I will cut of thy horses out of the midst of thee, and I will destroy thy chariots, and I will cut of the cities of thy land, and throw down all thy strongholds; and I will cut off witchcrafts out of thy hand, and thou shalt have no more soothsayers; thy graven images I will also cut off, and thy standing images out of the midst of thee, and thou shalt no more worship the works of thy hands; and I will pluck up thy groves out of the midst of thee; so will I destroy thy cities. And it shall come to pass that all lyings, and deceivings, and envyings and strifes, and priestcrafts, and whoredoms, shall be done away. For it shall come to pass, saith the Father, that at that day whosoever will not repent and come unto my beloved Son, them will I cut off from among my people, O house of Israel; and I will execute vengeance and fury upon them, even as upon the heathen, such as they have not heard."

"But if they will repent, and hearken unto my words, and harden not their hearts, I will establish my church among them, and they shall come in unto the covenant, and be numbered among this the remnant of Jacob unto whom I have given this land for their inheritance, and they shall assist my people the remnant of Jacob, and also, as many of the house of Isreal as shall come, that they may build a city, which shall be called the New Jerusalem; and then shall they assist my people that they may be gathered in, who are scattered upon all the face of the land, in unto the New Jeruselem. And then shall the power of heaven come down among them; and I also will be in the midst; and then shall the work of the Father commence at that day, even when this gospel shall be preached among the remnant of this people. Verily I say unto you, at that day shall the work of the Father commence among all the dispersed of my people; yea, even the tribes which have been lost, which the Father hath led away out of Jerusalem. Yea, the work shall commence among all the dispersed of my people with the Father, to prepare the way whereby they may come unto me."

From Orson Pratt's work, "New Jerusalem," page 6, we glean the following: "Ye are called to bring to pass the gathering of mine elect, for mine elect hear my voice and harden not their hearts; wherefore, the decree hath gone forth from the Father, that they shall be gathered in unto one place upon the face of this land, to prepare their hearts, and be prepared in all things against the day when tribulation and desolation are sent forth upon the wicked; for the hour is nigh and the day soon at hand when the earth is ripe; and all the proud and they that do wickedly, shall be as stubble and I will burn them up saith the Lord of Hosts, that wickedness shall not be upon the earth."

In December, 1830, the Lord gave a commandment unto the Saints in the State of New York, to remove to the State of Ohio.—(Sec. LVIII, par. 2.) Shortly after this the church commenced fulfilling this requirement, and within the short space of a few months, the majority of them were comfortably situated in the northern portions of Ohio. In February, 1831, the Saints were commanded to ask the Lord, and he would in due time reveal unto them the place where the New Jerusalem shoud be built, and where the Saints should eventually be gathered in one.—(Sec. XIII, par. 3, 10, 17, 18.)

On the 7th of March, 1831, the Saints were commanded to gather up their riches with one heart and one mind, to purchase an inheritance which the Lord should point out to them. In this revelation there were many predictions of a very important nature revealed. The inheritance, which was to be pointed out to them, and which they were to purchase, was to be the place of the New Jerusalem or Zion.—(Sec. XV., par. 12, 13, 14; also sec. LXIV. par. 2.)

In June following the Lord commanded between twenty and thirty of the elders to journey westward two by two, preaching the word and building up branches of the church wherever the people would receive their testimony. These elders were to take different routes, and meet together in the capacity of a conference in the western parts of Missouri, In this revelation the Lord said, that inasmuch as his elders were faithful, the land of their inheritance should be made known unto them; and also informed them that it was then in posession of their enemies. — (Sec. LXVI, par. 1, 2, 9.)

In this same month a small branch of the church, called the Colesville branch, who had emigrated from the State of New York to Ohio, where they had been for a few weeks, were commanded to remove to the western borders of Missouri, near the Lamanites.—(Sec. LXVIII, par. 2, 3.)

Joseph Smith and several of the elders arrived at Independence, Jackson County, Missouri, about the middle of July. Soon after their arrival, a revelation was given pointing out Independence as the central place for the city, and the place for the temple a short distance west of the court house.—(Sec. XXVII, par. 1.)

In this same revelation, the Saints were informed that it was wisdom to purchase the land throughout the country, that they might obtain it for an everlasting inheritance. Sidney Gilbert was appointed by revelation as an agent for the church; to receive money to buy land for the benefit of the Saints. Edward Partridge, who had previously been ordained a bishop with the assistance of his two counsellors, was commanded to divide to the Saints their inheritances according to their families. The bishop and the agent were also commanded to make preparations for the Colesville Saints, then on their way from the state of Ohio, that they might upon their arrival, be planted in their inheritances."

We quote the following from the Book of Mormon:

"Behold, the Lord hath shewn unto me great and mavelous things concerning that which must shortly come at that day when these things shall come forth among you. Behold, I speak unto you as if ye were present, and yet ye are not. But behold, Jesus Christ hath shewn you unto me, and I know your doing; and I know that ye do walk in the pride of your hearts; and there are none, save a few only, who do not lift themselves up in the pride of their hearts, unto the wearing of very fine apparel unto envying, and strifes, and malice, and persecutions, and all manner of iniquities: and your churches, yea, even every one, have become polluted because of the pride of your hearts. For behold, ye do love money, and your substances, and and your fine apparel, and the adorning of your churches, more than ye love the poor and the needy the sick and the afflicted. O ye polutions, ye hypocrites ye teachers, why sell yourselves for that which will canker, why have ye polluted the holy church of God? Why are ye ashamed to take upon you the name of Christ? Why do you not think that greater is the value of an endless happiness than that misery which never dies, because of the praise of the world? Why do ye adorn yourselves with that which hath no life, and yet suffer the hungry, and the needy, and the naked, and sick, and the afflicted to pass by you, and notice them not? Yea, why do you build up your secret abominations to get gain, and cause the widows should morn before the Lord, and also orphans to mourn before the Lord; and also the blood of their fathers and their husbands to cry unto the Lord from the ground, for vengeance upon your heads? Behold, the sword of vengeance hangeth over you; and the time soon cometh that he avengeth the blood of the Saints upon you, for he will not suffer their cries any longer.

Your words have been stout against me, saith the Lord. Yet ye say, what have we spoken against thee? Ye have said, it is vain to serve God, and what doth it profit that we have kept his ordinance, and that we have walked mournfully before the Lord of Hosts? And now we call the proud happy; yea, they that work wickedness are set up; yea, they that tempt God are even delivered.

Then they that feared the Lord spake often one to another, and the Lord hearkened and heard; and a book of remembrance was written before him for them that feared the Lord, and that thought upon his name. And they shall be mine, saith the Lord of Hosts, in that day when I make up my jewels; and I will spare them, as a man spareth his son that serveth him. Then shall we return and discern between the righteous and the wicked, between him that serveth God, and him that serveth him not. For behold, the day cometh that shall burn as an oven; and all the proud, yea, and all that do wickedly, shall be stubble: and the day that cometh shall burn them up, saith the Lord of Hosts, that it shall leave them neither root nor branch.

But unto you that fear my name, shall the Son of Righteousness arise with healing in his wings; and ye shall go forth and grow up as calves in the stall. And ye shall tread down the wicked; for they shall be ashes under the soles of thy feet in the day that I shall do this, saith the Lord of Hosts. Remember ye the law of Moses my servant, which I commanded unto him in Horib for all Israel, with the statutes and judgments. Behold, I will send Elijah the prophet before the coming of the great and dreadful day of the Lord; and he shall turn the heart of the fathers to the children, and the heart of the children to their fathers, lest I come and smite the earth with a curse."

Isaiah 1: 19-31. "If ye be willing and obedient, ye shall eat the good of the land: but if ye refuse and rebel, ye shall be devoured by the sword: for the mouth of the Lord hath spoken it.

How is the faithful city become an harlot! it was full of judgment; righteousness lodged in it; but now murderers. Thy silver has become dross. thy wine mixed with water: thy princes are rebellious, and companions of thieves: every one loveth gifts, and followeth after rewards: they judge not the fatherless, neither doth the cause of the widow come unto them. Therefore saith the Lord, the Lord of Hosts the mighty One of Israel, Ah, I will ease me of mine adversaries, and avenge me of mine enemies; and I will turn my hand upon thee, and purely purge away thy dross, and take away all thy tin: and I will restore thy judges as at the first, and thy counsellors as at the beginning: afterward thou shalt be called, the city of righteousness, the faithful city. Zion shall be redeemed with judgment, and her converts with righteousness.

And the destruction of the transgressors and of the sinners shall be together, and they that forsake the Lord shall be consumed. For they shall be ashamed of the oaks which ye have desired, and ye shall be confounded for the gardens which ye have chosen. For ye shall be as an oak whose leaf fadeth, and as a garden that hath no water. And the strong shall be as tow, and the maker of it as a spark, and they shall both burn together, and none shall quench them."

Farther, in relation to the work of the Lord, we quote from the Book of Mormon: "Wo unto them that call evil good and good evil; that put darkness for light and light for darkness; that put bitter for sweet and sweet for bitter! Wo unto the wise in their own eyes, and prudent in their own sight! Wo unto the mighty to drink wine, and men of strength to mingle strong drink; who justify the wicked for reward, and take away the righteousness of the righteous from him! Therefore, as the fire devoureth the stubble, and the flame consumeth the chaff, their root shall be rottenness, and their blossoms shall go up as dust; because they have cast away the law of the Lord of Hosts, and despised the Holy One of Israel. Therefore is the anger of the Lord kindled against his people, and he hath stretched forth his hand against them, and hath smitten them; and the hills did tremble, and their carcasses were torn in the midst of the streets. For all this his anger is not turned away, but his hand stretched out still."

"And it shall come to pass, that the Lord God shall bring forth unto you the words of a book, and they shall be the words of them that have slumbered. And behold the book shall be sealed: and in the book shall be a revelation from God, from the beginning of the world to the ending thereof. Wherefore, because of the things which are sealed up, the things which are sealed shall not be delivered in the day of the wickedness and abomination of the people. Wherefore the book shall be kept from them. But the book shall be delivered unto a man, and he shall deliver the words of the book, which are the words of those who have slumbered in the dust; but the words which are sealed he shall not deliver, neither shall he deliver the book."

"'And again it shall come to pass, that the Lord shall say unto him that shall read the words that shall be delivered him, forasmuch as this people draw near unto me with their mouth, and with their lips do honor me, but have removed their hearts far from me, and their fear towards me is taught by the precepts of men, therefore, I will proceed to do a marvellous work among this people, yea, a marvellous work and a wonder: ' for the wisdom of their wise and learned shall perish, and the understanding of their prudent shall be hid. And wo unto them that seek deep to hide their counsil from the Lord.

And their works are in the dark; and they say, who seeth us, and who knoweth us? And they also say, surely, your turning of things upside down shall be esteemed as the potter's clay. But behold, I will shew unto them, saith the Lord of Hosts, that I know all their works. For shall the work say of him that made it, he made me not? Or shall the thing framed say of him that framed it, he had no understanding? But behold, saith the Lord of Hosts, I will shew unto the children of men that it is not yet a very little while and Lebanon shall be turned into a fruitful field; and the fruitful field shall be esteemed as a forest. And in that day shall the deaf hear the word of the book, and the eyes of the blind shall see out of obscurity and out of darkness, and the meek also shall increase, and their joy shall be in the Lord, and the poor among men shall rejoice in the Holy One of Israel. For assuredly as the Lord liveth they shall see that the terrible one is brought to nought, and the scorner is consumed, and all that watch for iniquity are cut off; and they that make a man an offender for a word and lay a snare for him that reproveth in the gate, and turn aside the just for a thing of nought. Therefore, thus saith the Lord, who redeemed Abraham, concerning the house of Jacob, Jacob shall not now be ashamed, neither shall his face now wax pale. But when he seeth his children, the work of my hands, in the midst of him, they shall sanctify my name, and sanctify the Holy One of Jacob, and shall fear the God of Israel. They also that erred in spirit shall come to understanding, and they that murmured shall learn doctrine."

THE SIX FEMALE ARCHITECTS.

Q.—Who were the six female architects mentioned in Scripture, and what is the name of the edifice which they have erected in the material universe?

A.—1. Eve was the great architect of death and misery by an improper marriage relation. Gen. 3: 12.

2. Mary was the architect of life and the resurrection by a proper marriage relation. Her husband knew her not till the child was born and weaned. Matt. 1: 25.*

3. Leah. 4. Rachel. 5. Bilhah. 6. Zilpah.

The four last named females being in a proper marriage relation to Jacob, who wrestled with God in square holds, God told him his seed should be as the dust of the earth in number, in them should all the families of the earth be blessed. Gen. 28: 14. These four wives of Jacob are the architects of twelve sons. These twelve sons are the controlers of the twelve portals of the Zodiac: in the east, *first* the *ram*, the head, *Aries*, the house of Joseph, Joseph having two portions, being one of the twelve patriarchs he has the blessing of the womb and the breast. This is a part of the first portion. Gen. 49: 25 His second portion is to give the sun his light, being of the same order as Uralics, self-luminous, he rules the sun in the first portal and first house, *Abib*, or April. Gen. 37: 9.

Benjamin and Dan rule the other two eastern houses of the Zodiac. Rubin, Judah and Levi rule the three northern portals. The others west and south.

---

* "WOMAN IS THE ARCHITECT OF GOD'S NOBLEST WORK —Through all the period of gestation Nature works at the very citydel of life to build up the new temple of a living soul. If the organs of her body are defective and their functions feeble and inharmonious, Nature builds but a frail structure, that—failing to answer the proper objects and ends of life—is doomed to a brief existence of suffering and to perish prematurely. This is the sad history of millions of human beings, imperfectly generated, and born of mothers whom constitutional weakness and disease had rendered unworthy to assume the responsibility of parents.

When Gentiles die there are no comets seen, the heavens rejoice over the death of the Zion, the remnant or the priesthood of God.

All things, good and evil, that have a creation are first created in the mind of the mediumizer, or creator, by the free or absolute will of the medium, and through the camera or eye the recording of the image on the Zodiac, or ground plate, which is the power of remembrance, is accomplished. The transmission of the image by the generative organs in the proper order of marriage is the creative power; but if the female receive the image in the improper order of marriage, she becomes an excreator.

The name of the edifice erected by the six females is, *Solar System*.

In the grand circle of the Zodiac, is arranged, by the will (which is eventuality, causuality and comparison), in eternity, that which will take place in time, in the astronomical and prophetic order of the two great governing principles of the universe; namely, the self-indulging order of an Adam, an aristocratic government, and the self-sacrificing order of a Christ, a theocratic government.

After the flood the heaven was separated from the earth and the dragon gives his seat, which was the earth, and his power to the beast with seven heads and ten horns and two little horns. Rev. 13, and 17th chapters.

The Prophet Daniel was shown the world under aristocratic rule in his night vision. Dan. 7. God sends the Angel Gabriel from the courts of Glory to give Daniel understanding with regard to the end of aristocratic or Gentile rule of government on this planet. He instructs Daniel as to the seven great astronomical signs of the 2300 days divided into seven periods, at the end of which time the Gentile rule should end; viz. 2300 years after 400 B. C.

The Angel Gabriel says to Daniel, "Now I am come to make thee understand what shall befall *thy* people in latter-days, for yet the vision is for many days." Dan. 10: 14.

The *first* division of time is 62 weeks or 434 years The signs pertaining to this division of time are, 1st the going forth of the Decree of Artaxerxes; 2nd, Star of Bethleham; 3rd, the birth of the Messiah; 4th, the Temple; 5th, the supper; 6th, crucifixion of the Messiah.

The *second* division of time is 7 Weeks, or 49 years. The signs pertaining to this division of time are; 1st, the resurrection; 2nd, the assention; 3rd, the destruction of Jerusalem.

The *third* division of time is 70½ weeks, or 493 years. The signs pertaining to this division are; 1st, the spreading of the abomination of dessolation; 2nd, the man-child taken unto God; 3rd, the woman, or church, going into the wilderness. The weeks of Daniel ends here.

The *fourth* division of time is 1260 days or years. The signs pertaining to this division are; 1st, the tortures of Pagan Rome; 2nd, the tortures of Christian Rome; 3rd, the discovery of the new world; 4th, Pilgrim Fathers; 5th, the opening up of a new dispensation; 6th, the meeting of the grand council; 7th, the chariot of heaven bearing the mothers of Zion to the earth.

The *fifth* division of time is the last 30 years of the 1290 days, or years, of Daniel. The signs pertaining to this division are; 1st, the birth of the man-child; 2nd, the appearance of the Father and Son; 4th, the driving from Mossouri; 5th, the children at the mother's grave; 6th, the mother appearing to the children.

The *sixth* division of time is the last 45 years of the 1335 days, or years of Daniel. The signs pertaining to this division are; 1st, the reorganization of the apostolic power; 2nd, the keys received in the Kirtland Temple; 3rd, the assassination in the Carthage Jail; 4th, the Utah war; 5th, the year of Jubilee in 1880.

The *seventh* division of time is the last 17 years of the 2300 days, or years, of Daniel. The signs pertaining to this division are; 1st, the canceling of the debts of the people ($500,000); 2nd, the restoration of the higher law in 1882; 3rd, the gathering of the Zion of God; 4th, the coming of the Ancient of Days; 5th, the standing up of Micheal, the Mighty Prince, for his people at the great time of trouble at the end of the last 17 years of the 2300 years, or the year 1896, which is 1900 years after the birth of Christ.

Artaxerxes being the fifth king of the fourth head of the beast, the decree that began, of 2300 days, was ushered in on the 20th year of his reign, which begins the 62 weeks 400 years before the birth of the Messiah.

The rule of the Gentiles will continue from the going forth of the decree 2300 years, but "at the time appointed their end shall be." Dan. 12.

The above signs will be shown by illustrations from the best artists, through the Sterioptican Lantern on the screen at our evening lectures.

In the new creation Noah and Shem formed a theocratic government, on the ruins of which Nimrod, a descendant of Ham, formed an aristocratic government, which is the *first head* of the beast that came out of the sea with seven heads and ten horns, referred to in Rev. 13.

"And Cush begat Nimrod: he began to be a

mighty one in the earth. He was a mighty hunter before the Lord: wherefore it is said, 'even as Nimrod the mighty hunter before the Lord. And the beginning of his kingdom was Babel, and Erech, and Accad, and Calneh, in the land of Shinar. Out of that land went forth Ashur, and builded Nineveh and the city Rehoboth and Calah, and Resen between Nineveh and Calah: the same is a great city." Gen. 10: 8-12.

"That position of the earth upon which the City of Enoch was built, which was located where now flows the waters of the Gulf of Mexico, after being separated from the earth, caused such changes to take place, both in the position occupied by the land and the sea, with the changes wrought by the great earthquake which took place at the time of the flood, that instead of being in a position floating over the spot from whence it was taken, was in the days of Nimrod observed to be a few miles above that portion of the earth called the East Plains of *Shinar*. This discovery being made, the Devil put it into the hearts of Nimrod and his people to unite this city again with the earth.

The Book of Mormon page 446 verse 28, says: 'And also it is that same being who put it into the hearts of the people to build a tower sufficiently high to get to heaven.' Hence the building of the tower, and the reason for selecting the desolate and sandy East Plains of Shinar. Here also were immense stratas of clay from which bricks were manufactured to build this immense structure. They called the land and city floating over them Heaven, the place where the Gods dwelt. The Book of Mormon, in referring to this city, calls it the Holy Sanctuary of the Lord which should come down out of heaven."—*Prophetic History page 3*.

Pharoah is the *second head* of the beast.

The *third head* of the beast is the Babylonian government under Nebuchadnezzar, the first king, the head of gold mentioned in the dream of the image. The time of the prophetic dreams are, as given in Prophetic History page 9, as follows:

"*First.*—The dream of Nebuchadnezzar, of the Great Image in the 2nd year of his reign 586 B. C.

Second.—The vision of the four beasts that came up out of the sea, in the 1st year of the reign of Nabonid, called in Scripture Belshazzar, being in the 48th year from the dream of the image and 538 B. C.

Third.—The vision of the Ram and He-goat in the 3rd year of Belshazzar's reign, being in the 51st year from the dream of the image and 535 B. C.

Fourth.—The vision of the Angel Gabriel and time of the Messiah the prince, being in the 1st year of the reign of Cyaxares, called in Scripture, Darius the Mede, and 66 years from the time of the dream of the great image, 18 years from the vision of the four beasts, and 15 years from the time of the vision of the ram and he-goat Total time of captivity from the dream of the image 67 years. Darius the Mede reigned but 2 years, when Cyrus ascended the throne. In the 1st year of the reign of Cyrus the Babylonian captivity ended."

At three different times the Angel Gabriel came to instruct Daniel. 1st, In the third year of the reign of Belshazzar, when he instructs him of the 2300 days. (Dan. 8: 16.) 2nd, In the first year of Darius he instructs him of the weeks. (Dan 9: 21.) 3rd, He instructs Daniel of the 1290 days and the 1335 days. (Dan. 12: 11.)

The *Fourth head* of the beast is the Medes and Persians.

The *Fifth head* is the Macedonians under Alexander the Great.

The *Sixth head* of the beast is the Romans. Prophtic History page 49 says: "Rome was built upon seven hills. Her founder and first King was Romulus, who reigned for 37 years, died 714 B. C.

Numa Pompilius	"	43	" "	672 "
Tullis Hastilius	"	32	" "	640 "
Aneus Martius	"	24	" "	616 "
Lucius T. Priscus	"	38	" "	578 "
Servius Tullius	"	44	" "	534 "
Lucius Tarquinius	"	25	" "	599 "

Tarquinius was the last of the Roman kings. The Kingdom of Rome, having existed for 245 years, entered in and upon the foundation of a Republic, 509 years B. C.; seven kings having reigned upon the seven hills during the 245 years mentioned.

This Roman power descended from Japheth, the son of Noah; and hence was the Gentile nation spoken of in prophecy unto whom the Son of God was delivered. The Savior confirms their origin: 'And Jesus going up to Jerusalem took the twelve desciples apart in the way, and said unto them, behold we go up to Jerusalem; and the Son of man shall be betrayed unto the chief priests and unto the scribes, and they shall condemn him to death, and shall deliver him to the Gentiles to mock, and to scourge and to crucify him; and on the third day he shall rise again.' Matt. 20: 17."

The *Seventh head* is the Carthagenians, as shown in the following quotation: "And there are seven kings, five are fallen, and one is, [Romans] and the other is not yet come, [Carthagenians] and when he cometh he must continue a short space." Rev. 17:10.

The Romans redeemed their power with iron force instead of paying a tribute of gold.

The figure 7 is a significant figure. In these 7 heads are embodied the 7 orders of government: 1st domestic, 2nd combative. 3rd social, 4th moral, 5th recollective, 6th perceptive, 7th regulative. These 7 orders of government under the will, which is eventuality, causuality and comparison, is, in the perfect self-luminous man, the centre of all power good and evil, a centre without a circumference; these are the seven eyes that see all things; the seven lamps that enlighteneth all things; the seven spirits that are in and through all things; these are, phrenologically speaking, the seven groups of organs. See Zack. 4; Rev, 1.

The Messiah was put to death on the 6th day of the first month in the year, in the house of Joseph, or portal of April, which is the first and not the fourth, *aries*, the ram, the head, or ruler of that house, the cepter having departed from Judah in the fifth house, the lion in the portal of August, in the year 33.

On the 10th of the following April, for the first time in the second creation, salvation was offered to the Gentiles by the Holy Ghost. Acts 10: 44-45; B. of M. III Nephi 9: 9.

The Blind Iron Horn of the Gentiles, the fourth beast, or sixth head, began its rule by trampling on the laws of nations and the virtue of females. Rather than to have ten females for one male as the former nations, they reversed it and gave one female for ten males, the increase of their government not depending on parental government.

Having disposed of the seven heads and the blind little horn of the Gentiles, we shall now take up the ten kingdoms, or horns, or toes. Bishop Loyd in his interpretation exhibits the following list. as also the time of their rise:

1 Huns	356 A. D.		6 Sueves and Alans	407
2 Ostrogoths	377	"	7 Burgundians near	407
3 Visogoths	378	"	8 Herules & Rugians	476
4 Franks	407	"	9 Saxons, about	476
5 Vandals	407	"	10 Longobards	476

The names of the ten horn kingdoms that were to exist in the dominion of the beast when the God of Heaven should set up a Kingdom never more to be thrown down are given in Prophetic History, page 117, as follows:

1 Italy born	476, A. D.	6 Portugal	born	1138,
2 France "	752,	7 Prussia	"	1139,
3 Belgium "	865,	8 Austro-Hungaria		1153,
4 England "	802,	9 Spain,	born	1471,
5 Holland "	922,	10 Greece	"	1789.

As the blind little horn of the Roman government, or Gentile power, at the beginning of their rule changed their polititics as they changed clothing, and in a base, brutal and bloody manner trampled upon the virtue of the females; so will the seeing little horn, which is the government of the United States, close the rule of the Gentiles in like manner, as shown in the following quotation:

"And of the ten horns that were in his head and of the others which came up and before whom three fell, even of that horn which had eyes and a mouth that speaks great things, whose look was more stout than his fellows; and I beheld, and the same horn made war with the saints and prevailed against them until the Ancient of Days came, and judgment was given to the Saints of the Most High, and the time came that the Saints possessed the Kingdom." Dan. 7: 20-22.

Who colonized the land of America? The people from the ten kidgdoms. Who built the villages, towns and cities of America? The people from the ten kingdoms. Who fought the battles of the United States? The people from the ten kingdoms. Who organized the Congress of the United States? The people from the ten kingdoms.

Please read the whole of Prov. VII. carefully. This is the order of things sought to be introduced by the Christian friends of the "Mormons."

"And in the days of these kings shall the God of heaven set up a Kingdom, which shall never be destroyed, and the Kingdom shall not be left to other people, but it shall break in pieces and consume all these kingdoms and it shall stand forever." Dan. 2: 44. This is done by the Zion of God, whose mothers were called ordained and set apart in the grand council of the heavens to come to the earth on and after the year 1782, to be the mothers of the Zion of God, or the Priesthood of God, that was to be born among the nations of the Gentiles in this dispensation for the salvation of all things. These are the remnant spoken of by the prophets. These are the pure in heart. These are the elect of God, that He scattered among the Gentiles that He might bring salvation to all. These are to be gathered to one place on the land of America by the ordinances of the priesthood, to form a great grand center, a nucelus of truth and virtue around which will be gathered the truth and virtue of this Solar System in their place and order. See Heb. 2: 7, Nephi 6, Doc. and Cov. Sec. 84-113.

Seeing that God has gathered His Zion, His Priesthood, His Chosen Ones to Utah in fulfillment of all the prophecies of His Ancient Prophets, the question now is, what is He going to do with them? Is He going to fulfill His former plans? or is He going to permit the little horn to eat them up without salt?

In the second creation, 2348 B. C., the covenant was made with Noah, not only for himself, but also for his posterity, therefore it is our right, as his children, to know what *was* that covenant and through which of his seed were we to have a part in that covenant.

An agreement or contract is in its very nature a *promise*, as we may see at a glance. There can be no agreement made unless a promise is made; this is so in the very nature of things. When one agrees to do a thing he at the same time *promises* to do it, and so Mr. Webster defines *promise* to mean: "A declaration by one person to another, which bids him who makes it to do or forbear a specified act."

These were the *conditions* of the covenant or contract. Here was a mutual agreement entered into, to do or forbear specified acts. The *acts* to be done or forborne were what the voice of the Lord commanded, which the people promised to obey.

This covenant consists of many parts, it being a perfect theocratic government that God gave to Noah. 1st, To multiply and replenish the earth. Gen. 9: 1. 2nd, That man was the Lord of creation. 3rd, That man was to love his neighbor as himself. 4th, That labor was to be equalized among all his children. 5th, The earth with all that belong to it be the property of all equally, that belong to it and not the exclusive property of any particular class, party or generation.

It is through the seed of Shem that those blessings come to the human family. Gen. 20: 21. Upon the ruins of this theocratic government did Nimrod raise the black flag of piracy and erect an aristocratic government of brute force. Josephus says:

"Now it was Nimrod who excited them to such an affront and contempt of God He was the grandson of Ham, the son of Noah,—a bold daring man, and of great strenth of hand. He persuaded them not to ascribe it to God, as if it was through his means they were happy, but to believe that it was their own courage which procured that happiness. He also gradually changed the government into tyrany,—seeing no other way of turning men from the fear of God, but to bring them into a constant dependence upon his power. He also said he would be revenged on God, if he should have a mind to drown the world again; for that he would build a tower too high for the waters to be able to reach! and that he would avenge himself on God for destroying their forefathers!

Now the multitude were very ready to follow the determination of Nimrod, and to esteem it a piece of cowardice to submit to God; and they built a tower, neither sparing any pains, nor being in any degree negligent about the work; and, by reason of the multitude of hands employed in it, it grew very high, sooner than any one could expect; but the thickness of it was so great, and it was so strongly built, that thereby its great hight seemed, upon the view, to be less than it really was. It was built of burnt brick, cemented together with mortar, made of bitumen, that it might not be liable to admit water. When God saw that they acted so madly, he did not resolve to destroy them utterly, since they were not grown wiser by the destruction of the former sinners; but he caused a tumult among them, by producing in them diverse languages; and caused that through the multitude of those languages they should not be able to understand one another. The place wherin they built the tower is now called *Babylon;* because of the confusion of that language which they redily understood before; for the Hebrews mean by the word *Babel*, confusion. The Sybil also makes mention of this tower, and of the confusion of the language, when she says thus:—'When all men were of one language, some of them built a high tower, as if they would thereby ascend up to heaven; but the gods sent storms of wind and overthrew the tower and gave every one his peculiar language; and for this reason it was that the city was called *Babylon*.' "

The origin of the *Gentiles* and the meaning of each order in the 2nd creation is as follows: The Gentiles have three different origins; 1st, Japheth, the son of Noah, was the father of seven nations of Gentiles that spread over part of Asia and Europe, (Gen. 9: 19, I. Josephus chap. 6.); 2nd, Canan, one of the sons of Ham was the father of eleven nations, (Gen. 10; Josepus 1st book chap. 6 verse 2.); 3rd, Esau, the son of Jacob was the father of seven nations, called the Edomites, (Gen. 36.) The true meaning of the Japheth order of Gentiles is a servant of love. Gen. 9: 27. The true meaning of the Canan order of Gentiles is a servant of slavery, a curse. Gen. 9:5. The true meaning of the Esau order of Gentiles is a servant of hate. Gen. 27: 41. With the Gentiles, according to their own statements in their works, nothing is eternal, all things have a beginning, even their own existence. Their system of optics is that no external object can become visible to us unless some rays of light proceed from them and fall upon our eyes. They say:

"When we look from an eminence on a clear day, and view the surrounding country. Every tree, yea every blade of grass, sends rays of light to the eyes, without which it would be impossible to see the beautiful verdure of the fields beneath. But is it not more wonderful still, that though we have two eyes, we do not see double. Remember further, that those objects which we see, are not only visible to us but other points. We are justly surprised at the number of rays which they transmit to so small a space as the pupil of the eye. The image of all outward objects is painted on the retina, upside down, and yet we see all things right, and in their real situation. Though the largest objects are painted on our eyes extremely small, yet we see every thing according to its real size. How does it happen, that when from the top of a tower we perceive thousands of houses below us in a large city, that each is painted so exactly in our eye, on a surface scarcely three times as large as the head of a pin? So many millions of rays coming through a small aperture, are united in the retina, which covers the bottom of the eye, without the least confusion; though they preserve among themselves the same order with the points of the objects from which they proceed. Nor is this all: look from the top of a mast upon a fleet in the open sea, in full sail; contemplate the sea itself, and how many millions of waves will you behold! and yet each of them, small as they are, reflect a mass of rays upon the eyes."

Ours is only to-day. Let us enjoy the beauties of nature for there is no to-morrow. The science of optics, the powers of visage and the mind creating system prove it: the image of the blade of grass is carried by the rays of light to the eye of the pregnant lady. The image passes through the pupil, is transversely thrown upon the retina byt he lens and fluids of the eye. The image of the blade of grass is picked up by the optic nerve and is transmitted to the brain of the pregnant lady, where it forms an impression. The impression creates a sensation; the sensation is formed into a conscientious thought; the thought is transformed into a soul by the laws of assimilation; the soul becomes the mind of the child and is the creature of the body, depending on the body for its existence, and when the body has finished its earthly carear the mind falls back upon the soul; the soul falls back upon the consiencious thought; the thought falls back on the sensation; the sensation falls back on the impression; the impression falls back on the image; the image is carried back to the blade of grass by the focalizing power of the eye. Thus the mind, the soul, the spirit and the body are disposed of in the most scientific manner by the great and learned Gentile friends of science.

The optical professors of to-day tell us that the eye is a self-regulating and self-focalizing camera that receives the rays of light from the object.

The ancient optical professors taught that the rays of light proceed from the eye to the object. This was the Plato and Euclid theory.

"We cannot create force. We can only take it as a gift from God. We find it everywhere in Nature; so that matter is not dumb, but full of inherent energy. A tiny drop of dew sparkling on a spire of grass is instinct with power: Gravity draws it to the earth; Chemical Afinity binds together the atoms of hydrogen and oxogen; Cohesion holds the molecules of water, and gathers the drop into a globe; Heat keeps it in the liquid form; Adhesion causes it to cling to the leaf. If the water be decomposed, Electricity will be set free; and from this, Heat, Light, Magnetism and Motion can be produced. Thus the commonest object becomes full of fascination to the scientific mind, since in it reside the mysterious force of Nature.

These various forces can be classified either as attractive or repellent. Under their influence the atoms or molecules resemble little magnets with positive and negative poles. They therefore approach or recede from one another, and so tend to arrange themselves according to some definite plan. "The atoms march in time, moving to the music of law." A crystal is but a specimen of "molecular architecture" built up by the forces with which matter is endowed. Forces continually ebb and flow, but the sum of energy through the universe remains the same. In time all the possible changes may be rung, and the various forms of energy subside into one uniformly-diffused heat-quiver, but in that will exist the representation of all the forces which now animate creation, and, as we believe, matter and force will perish only together.

The forces of Nature are strangely linked with our lives. Everywhere a Divine Hand is developing ideas tenderly and wonderously related to human needs. To the thoughtful mind all phenamena have a hidden meaning."

Such, Orson Pratt says: "Vague speculations, wild hypotheses, romance, fiction and every other kindred curse, handed down from the fathers, ought no longer to be considered a part of education. The memories of youthful students ought no longer to be overburdened with isolated facts in a science, when laws comprehending such facts are accessible. Facts may be useful in illustrating laws: but laws show why the facts exist. He, therefore, is truely educated in a science, who has understandingly acquired a knowledge of the laws on which the individual facts depend."

God created man in his own likeness; that is, the self-existing eternal intellectual man got a body in precisely the same manner as God got his body. Gen. 1. An eternal God, an eternal man, is the eternal hope of Shem, the father of all the children of Eber, the mother of the Hebrews, (Gen. 10: 21, Josephus book 1st chap. 6.) and the father of the children of the mother of Elem, Asher, Arphaxad, Lud and Aram, the fathers of the faithful and the true, (Gen. 10: 22.) supporters of the theocratic government of God, with Melchesidek, Abraham, Isaac, Jacob and the twelve tribes of Israel. These are the friends of the God of the Hosts of Israel. God ate, drank, walked, talked face to face and wrestled in square holds with his much married people.

The house of Jacob is a fire, the house of Joseph is a flame and the house of Esau is stubble. Obediah 1: 18. The Lord takes his prophets out of the children of Israel and his Nazarenes out of the young men of Israel. Amos 2: 11. Israel is a family of Gods and sons of Gods, that is their origin. The meaning of the word Israel, is self-luminous. The optical laws of Israel is that there *is* a to-morrow in which the action of to-day is felt. The spirit of God is eternal, the spirit of the Devil is eternal and the spirit of man is eternal, co-eternal the one with the other. The spirit of the Gods have the seven groups of organs, or seven eyes that see all things, the seven lamps that enlighteneth all things, the seven spirits that are in and around all things in space, infinitely extended, a centre without a circumference, the Holy Ghost, acting according to their own will, which is eventuality, causuality and comparison. Zac. 4, Rev. 1.

When the Gods take mortal bodies, in their incarnation their recollection of the past is taken from them by their submitting their will to the father, but when their perceptive powers are quickened by the observation of lawful ordinances it makes them mighty, for knowledge is power and union is strength.

Light regulates heat; heat regulates motion; motion regulates time; thus, the self-luminous man is the centre of time, motion, heat, light, knowledge and perception; and, as all that have a beginning are first created in the mind of the creator or mediumizer, the creator of each Solar System has imprinted upon his mind, by optical laws, the image of all the *first borns* of that creation, in animal life, mineral life, atmospheric life, vegetable life and the lives of soils, metals and waters.

In the self-luminous eternal sphere there is no such thing as a beginning but by a change of place, state or condition, the eternal man freely giving up his own will to another, becoming a baby by parental government; 1st in a spiritual state, 2nd in a temporal state.

The father of 144,000 first born, only begotten sons (as each of these sons must have 144,000 only begotten self-luminous females to be their wives to enable each son to do as his father done,) must be the father of 20,736,000,000 daughters in order to act honestly with the sons.

The Adam-God of this planet has to look after all the first creation before Noah, the twelve tribes of Israel and the seven heads, ten kings and two little horns of the Gentiles in the second creation. Gen. 3:22. The father and redeemer by a blood atonement of 144,000 Adam-Gods is a Lord Jesus Christ. The Father and glorifier of a Lord Jesus Christ is an Elohcim God, the great grand center of all light, and life, the ruler of all things in the immensity of space by the Spirit, the Holy Ghost, the other Comforter, or the rays of light and heat that is transmitted from His Luminous Person in straight lines in every direction throughout the immensity of space according to His infinite will, which is eventuality, causuality and comparison. Yet, when the Gods are in a mortal state, their natural body is the clothing of the spiritual body. The natural eye is the window for the seven spiritual eyes to see through when not in a magnetic state, trance state or state of vision.

All things that exist in space are, by the will power, under the government of one and either and each and all of these seven eyes; viz., 1st, the laws of force; 2nd, the laws of applying force; 3rd, the laws of energy; 4th, the laws of gravatation; 5th, the laws of affinity; 6th the laws of cohesion; 7th, the laws of adhesion.

Jacob, the great optical professor, knew that the organs of size, form and color, in the eternal spirit, would take observation through the natural eyes:

"And Jacob took him rods of green poplar, and of the hazel and chesnut tree; and pilled white streaks in them, and made the white appear which was in the rods. And he set the rods which he had pilled before the flocks in the gutters in the watering troughs when the flocks came to drink, that they should conceive when they came to drink. And the flocks conceived before the rods, and brought fourth cattle ringstreaked, speckled and spotted. And Jacob did separate the lambs, and set the faces of the flocks toward the ringstreaked, and all the brown in the flocks of Laban; and he put his own flocks by themselves, and put them not unto Laban's cattle. And it came to pass, whensoever the stronger cattle did conceive, that Jacob laid the rods before the eyes of the cattle in the gutters, that they might conceive among the rods. But when the cattle were feble, he put them not in: so the febler were Laban's, and the stronger Jacob's. And the man increased exceedingly, and had much cattle, and maid servants, and menservants, and camels, and asses." Gen. 30: 37-43.

The following from Josephus shows that God works in the same order:

"Now here one may wonder at the ill-will which men bear to us, and which they profess to bear on account of our despising that Deity which they pretend to honor; for if any one do but consider the fabric of the tabernacle, and take a view of the garments of the priests, and of those vessels which we make use of in our sacred ministrations, he will find that our legislator was a divine man and that we are unjustly reproached by others: for if any one do without prejudice, and with judgment, look upon these things, he will find they were every one made in way of imitation and representation of the univese. When Moses distinguished the tabernacle into three parts and allowed two of them to the priests, as a place accessible and common, he denoted the land and the sea, these being of general access to all; but he set apart the third divlsion for God.

The answers by the oracle of Urim and Thumim, which words signify *light* and *perfection*, or, as the Septuagent render them, *revelation* and *truth*, and denote nothing further, that I see, but the shining stones themselves, which are used, in this method of illumination, in revealing the will of God, after a peefect and true manner, to his people Israel: I say, these answers were not made by the shining of the precious stones, after an awkward manner, in the high-priest's brest-plate, as the modern Rabbins vainly suppose, for certainly the shining of the stones might preceed or accompany the oracle, without itself delivering that oricle, but rather by an audible voice from the mercy-seat between the cherubims. See Prideaux's connect, at the year 524. This oracle had been silent two hundred years, ever since the day of the last good high-priest of the family of the Maccabees, John Hyrcanus. Now it is here very well worth our observation, that the oracle before us was that by which God appeared to be present with, and gave directions to, his people Israel as their king, all the while they submitted to him in that capacity; and did not set over them such independent kings as governed according to their own wills and political maxims, instead of divine directions. Accordingly we meet with this oracle (besides angelic and prophetic admonitions) all along from the days of Moses and Joshua to the annointing of Saul, the first of the succession of the kings (Numb. 27: 21; Josh. 6: 6; Jud. 1: 1; 18: 4-31; 20: 18-28; 21: 1; 1 Sam. 1: 17, 18); nay, till Saul's rejection of the divine commands in the war with Amalek, when he took upon him to act as he thought fit (Sam. 14: 3-37), then this oracle left Saul entirely and accompanied David, who was annointed to succeed him, and who consulted God by it frequently, and complied with its directions constantly. Saul, indeed, long after his rejection by God, and when God had given him up to destruction for his disobedience, did once afterwards endeavor to consult God when it was too late; but God would not then answer him, neither by dreams, nor by Urim, nor by prophets. Nor did any of David's successors, the kings of Judah, consult God by this oracle, that we know of, till the very Babylonish captivity itself, when those kings were all at an end; they taking upon them, I suppose, too much of despotic power and royalty, and too little owning the God of Israel for the supreme King of

Israel, though a few of them consulted the prophets sometimes, and were answered by them. At the return of the two tribes, without the return of the kingly government, the restoration of this oracle was expected (Neh. 7: 63; 1. Esd. 5: 40; 1 Mac. 4: 46; 14: 41). And indeed it may seem to have been restored for sometime after the Babylonish captivity, at least in the days of that excellent high-priest, John Hyrcanus, who was esteemed as a king, a priest and prophet; and who foretold several things that came to pass accordingly; but about the time of his death this oracle quite ceased, and not before. The following high-priests now puting diadems upon their heads, and ruling according to their own will, and by their own authority, like the other kings of the Pagan countries about them; so that while the God of Israel was allowed to be the supreme King of Israel, and his directions to be their authentic guides, God gave them such directions as their supreme king and governor; and they were properly under a theocracy."

Q.—Who is man?

A.—Man is an eternal self-existing self-seeing being. "The spirit of man is eternal," says Joseph Smith (Mill. Star Vol. 17, page 311; Times and Seasons Vol. 5, page 612-615). We quote the following from Mill. Star Vol. 5, page 90, Joseph Smith's words:

"I have another subject to dwell upon, and it is impossible for me to say much, but I shall just touch upon them; for time will not permit me to say all, so I must come to the resurrection of the dead, the soul, the mind of man, the immortal spirit. All men say God created it in the beginning. The very idea lessens man in my estimation; I do not believe the doctrine—I know better. Hear it all ye ends of the world, for God has told me so. I will make a man appear a fool before I get through, if you don't believe it. I am going to tell of things more noble—we say that God himself is a self-existing God; who told you so? it is correct enough; but how did you get it into your heads? Who said that man did not exist in like manner upon the same principles? How does it read in the Hebrew? It don't say so in the Hebrew, it says God made man out of the earth, and put into him Adam's spirit, and so became a living body.

The mind of man is as immortal as God himself. I know that my testimony is true, hence, when I talk to these mourners; what have they lost? They are only separated from their bodies for a short season; their spirits existed co-equal with God, and they now exist in a place where they converse together the same as we do on the earth. Is it logic to say that a spirit is immortal, and yet have a beginning? Because if a spirit have a beginning it will have an end: good logic. I want to reason more on the spirit of man, for I am dwelling on the body of man, on the subject of the dead. I take my ring from my finger and liken it to the mind of man, the immortal spirit, because it has no beginning. Suppose you cut it in two; but as the Lord lives there would be an end. All the fools, learned and wise men, from the beginning of creation, who say that man had a beginning, proves that he must have an end, and then the doctrine of anihilation would be true. But, if I am right, I might with boldness proclaim from the house-tops that God never did have power to create the spirit of man at all. God himself could not create himself: intelligence exists upon a self-existent principle, it is a spirit from age to age, and there is no creation about it.

All the spirits that God ever sent into the world are susceptible of enlargment. The first principles of man are self-existent with God: that God himself finds himself in the midst of spirits and glory, because he was greater, and because he saw proper to institute laws, whereby the rest could have a privilege to advance like himself, that they might have one glory upon another, in all knowledge, power and glory, in order to save the world of spirits. I know that when I tell you these words of eternal life, that are given to me, I know you taste it, and I know you believe it. You say honey is sweet and so do I. I can also taste the spirit of eternal life; I know it is good, and, when I tell you of these things, that were given me by inspiration of the Holy Spirit, you are bound to receive it as sweet, and I rejoice more and more."

Q.—When did Joseph Smith become a prophet?

A.—"I [Brigham Young] can tell you. When he became an Apostle, years and years before he had the right of holding the keys of the Aaronic Priesthood. He was a prophet before he was baptised." *Times and Seasons*, Oct. 6, 1844.

Q.—Is the apostle to ordain an apostle to be an high-priest?

A.—"To do so would be an insult to the priesthood." *Jour. of Dis.* Vol. 1, page 139.

Q.—What keys do the Twelve Apostles hold?

A.—Every key needful to save in the Celestial Kingdom was given to the Twelve Apostles." *Mill. Star*, Vol. 10, page 113. At a public meeting in Nauvoo, Brigham Young said: "The Twelve hold the keys of the Priesthood." *T. and S.* Vol. 5, 638. "Joseph Smith gave the Twelve Apostles all the keys of the Kingdom saying, 'if they kill me, I have given you all.'" *T. and S.* Vol. 5, p. 651. "The

Twelve are the proper persons to lead the Church." Wm. Marks, Dec. 9. 1844. "God has chosen us, the Twelve, to be special witnesses." Wm. Smith see *The Prophet*, Sep. 4, 1844.

Q.—What rights appertain to man?

A.—The rights of man are manifold, but may be comprehended in the four following—viz., his right to life, his right to self-government, his right to acquire and to hold property, and his right to the free exercise of his mental and physical powers, so that the rights of others are not infringed thereby.

Q.—Is not the land private property?

A.—No.

Q.—Why not?

A.—Because the Lord hath forbid. "The land shall not be sold forever, for the land is mine, for ye are strangers and sojourners with me." Lev. 25: 23.

Q.—Do you say the land cannot become private property?

A.—The land is public property, and cannot become the exclusive property of any distinct party or class.

Q.—What is the reason why the land cannot become the exclusive property of any distinct party or class?

A.—Because it is the foundation of all labor, and the raw material from which all wealth is produced; and all men having the same right to, and the same right to preserve it, it must therefore be evident, that the exclusive possession of it by any distinct party or class would prevent others from exercising the same rights and privileges as those who would be in the possession of it.

"Over a century ago Benj. Franklin asserted that in the condition of the world then, without steam and machinery, four hours from each capable would be enough, daily, to do all useful work. Twenty years ago statisticians ascertained that in the state of machinery then, three hours a day would be enough. Doubtless to-day, with the countless inventions since, two hours would do. But assuming as true now the calculation for twenty years ago, then each ten men, working three hours daily, in all thirty hours, would be able, as the results of their labor, to obtain for themselves such a share of the wealth production as would enable them to get, not only the necessaries of life, but to enjoy its luxuries and pleasures as well.

But if, of these ten men, one refused to do his share, and demanded support from the others, the nine left would have to work $3\frac{1}{3}$ hours per day. If 2 refused, the 8 must work $3\frac{3}{4}$ "

"	3	"	7	"	$4\frac{2}{7}$	"
"	4	"	6	"	5	"
"	5	"	5	"	6	"
"	6	"	4	"	$7\frac{1}{2}$	"
"	7	"	3	"	10	"
"	8	"	2	"	15	"

Here the limit of endurance is passed. As the average days work exacted from the toiler is now about twelve hours, it is plain that five men out of twenty really do all the useful work. Each of these five then support themselves, and three other men also. And as each family averages five, each wealth producer bestows food, shelter, clothing and all the concomitants of his civilization, generating millionaires and tramps upon twenty persons.

Q.—Do not those individuals who possess the land hold it by virtue of a superior right to do so?

A.—No.

Q.—How then did they acquire it?

A —The greatest portion of those hold it on account of their predecessors having driven the original inhabitants from it by brute force, while others hold it by virtue of a grant from the government and some by purchase.

Q.—Do not those individuals who procured it by conquest hold it justly?

A.—No; superior power, used in an improper manner, by brute force, cannot obtain superior rights they do not already possess, in justice.

Q.—Do not those who obtained it by virtue of a grant from the government hold it justly?

A.—No; governments have no exclusive rights but what are conferred upon them by the people, and no people can confer rights which they themselves do not possess.

Q.—Do those who acquired the land by purchase not hold it justly?

A.—No; they are upon a level with purchasers of stolen goods, who cannot hold what they have purchased; those who sell the land have no more right to it than the purchaser previous to purchasing.

Q.—What is meant by self-government?

A.—That every person has the right to say how he shall be governed.

Q.—Are the people of this country allowed the free exercise of that right?

A.—No; only a few.

Q.—Why are the great mass of the people deprived of the free exercise of this right?

A.—Partly on account of their own ignorance, and partly because a distinct class holds possession of the land.

Q.—By what means did those who have the power of making the laws, by which the people of this country are governed, acquire such power?

A.—The same means by which they got possession of the land—the possession of the land conferring the power upon them.

Q.—What benefit do they derive from making the laws?

A.—The same benefit which a highway robber derives from disarming the person he robs—viz., the power to retain what he has unjustly acquired, and also the power to acquire more in the same manner.

Q.—Is there no land monopoly, and a refined system of tyrany among the Latter-day Saints of Utah?

A.—The telestial gospel of Jesus Christ gathers all kinds to Utah, it being the separating place,

Q.—Is there not a priestcraft in the "Mormon" Church as well as all other churches?

A.—The "Mormon" Church is the only church of all churches in which you shall find priestcraft; priestcraft cannot exist where priesthood is not.

The following from Pres. John Taylor's discourse given in the *Deseret News*, Oct. 12, 1884, relates to this subject:

"'Behold there are many called, but few are chosen. And why are they not chosen?"—[here is the reason]—"Because their hearts are set so much upon the things of this world, and they aspire to the honors of men, that they do not learn this one lesson—That the rights of the Priesthood are inseparably connected with the powers of heaven, and that the powers of heaven cannot be controlled nor handled only upon the principles of righteousness. That they may be conferred upon us it is true; but when we undertake to cover our sins, or to gratify our pride, our vain ambition, or to exercise control, or dominion, or compulsion, upon the souls of the children of men, in any degree of unrighteousness, behold, the heavens will withdraw themselves; the spirit of the Lord is grieved; and when it is withdrawn, amen to the Priesthood or authority of that man. Behold! ere he is aware, he is left unto himself, to kick against the pricks; to persecute the Saints and to fight against God. We have learned by sad experience, that it is the nature and disposition of nearly all men, as soon as they get a little authority as they suppose, they will immediately begin to exercise unrighteous dominion.' Doc. and Cov. Sec. 121: 34-41.

Hear it you Elders of Israel, you Presidents of Stakes, you Bishops and men of authority, and you Elders everywhere! This is the reason men have departed from the truth and have apostatized.

'Hence many are called but few are chosen. No power or influence can or ought to be maintained by virtue of the Priesthood, only by persuation, by long suffering, by gentleness and meekness, and by love unfeigned; by kindness and pure knowledge, which shall greatly enlarge the soul without hypocrisy and without guile.'

This is the reason why so many have stumbled, and I will say still further that unless the Elders of Israel realize their position, whether they be Presidents of Stakes, or whether they be the Twelve, or the councilors of the Twelve or the First Presidency, or whether they be Bishops, or whether they hold any office of authority in the Church and Kingdom of God—no matter what position they may occupy, if they go to work to seek to aggrandise themselves at the expense of the Church and Kingdom of God, the Spirit of God will be withdrawn from them and they will be left as others have been left to "kick against the pricks" and to fight against God, and they will find their way to perdition instead of to the Celestial Kingdom of God."

Matt. 20: 25-28, says: "But Jesus called them unto him, and said, ye know that the princes of the Gentiles exercise dominion over them, and they that are great exercise authority upon them. But it shall not be so among you; but whosoever will be great among you, let him be your minister; and whosoever will be chief among you, let him be your servant: even as the Son of man came not to be ministered unto, but to minister, and to give his life a ransom for many."

Phil. 2: 1-8, says: "If there be, therefore, any consolation in Christ, if any comfort of love, if any fellowship of the Spirit, if any bowels and mercies, fulfil ye my joy, that ye be likeminded, having the same love, being of one accord, of one mind. Let nothing be done through strife or vainglory: but in lowliness of mind let each esteem others better than themselves. Look not every man on his own things, but every man also on the things of others. Let this mind be in you, which was also in Christ Jesus: who, being in the form of God, thought it not robbery to be equal with God: but made himself of no reputation, and took upon him the form of a servant, and was made in the likeness of men: and being found in fashion as a man, he humbled himself, and became obedient unto death, even the death of the cross."

Doc. and Cov. Sec. 1: 11-16, says: "Wherefore the voice of the Lord is unto the ends of the earth, that all that will hear may hear; prepare ye, prepare ye for that which is to come, for the Lord is nigh; and the anger of the Lord is kindled, and his sword is bathed in heaven, and it shall fall upon the inhabitants of the earth; and the arm of the Lord shall be revealed; and the day cometh, that they who will not hear the voice of the Lord, neither the voice of his servants, neither give head to the words of the prophets and apostles, shall be cut off from among the people: for they have strayed from mine ordinances, and have broken mine everlasting covenant; they seek not the Lord to establish his righteousness, but every man walketh in his own way, and after the image of his own god, whose image is in the likeness of the world, and whose substance is that of an idol, which waxeth old and shall perish in Babylon, even Babylon the great which shall fall."

A CHALLENGE.

Salt Lake City, July 17, 1885.
To *Joseph Smith, Jr., President of the Reorganized Church of Jesus Christ of Latter-day Saints.*

Sir—I am a liberal sustainer of all the branches of "Mormonism," or any other "ism" that has truth and sustains it, but the extraordinary nature of your pretensions, as given in your discourse of June 28, 1885, make it desirous of having their truth and validity inquired into fairly.

You claim that the Bible, Book of Mormon and Doctrine and Covenants are the foundation of salvation on which you base your organization I claim that, if Joseph Smith, Sen., brought salvation to the children of men in our day, it was abstract and independent of all books, and you are wrong in depending upon books for salvation.

You claim the right to the priesthood and apostleship, by choosing and authority of the laws embodied in the books. I claim that the fullness of the Priesthood is collected from the nations of the earth and is not conferable by temporal ordinances.

You claim that your organization is the Church of Jesus Christ of Latter-day Saints. I claim that the prophetic, mathmatical arrangements of all the drophets prove you to be wrong.

In order that the truth and validity of your pretensions may be fairly and publicly investigated, I challenge you to meet me in open public debate, with the understanding that politics, poligamy and the character of individuals shall not be discussed.

If you accept this challenge, the time, place and conditions can be arranged. A small entrance fee must be charged the public in order to defray necessary expenses. Yours respectfully,

ANGUS McDONALD, a free-thinker.

THE THREE BOOK SALVATION.

To the Editor of the *Herld*.

My challenge to Joseph Smith, Jr., President of the Reorganized Church, appearing in the *Hearld*, July 19th, being refused, I beg lief to occupy a short space in your columns, to show my grounds for the challenge. I will be as brief as possible.

From Jos. Smith's discourse of June 28th, published in the *Tribune* June 30th, we have these words: "He detailed the manner in which the reorganization took place. It began in 1851, with members who were identified with the church in Joseph's time—one branch at Jeffersonville, Wayne Co. Ill., organized by Thos. P. Green, and one near Balloit, Mo., and a number of the saints in Southern Wis. and Northern Ills. The movement began with these. They met together for prayer, and were directed by the spirit to take the book of Doctrine and Covenants, made preparation for and held a conference in June 1852, at which conference they passed a resolution indorsing the Bible, Book of Mormon and Doctrine and Covenants as the law to govern the church. They appointed a committee and elders who began laboring and holding conferences each year up to 1860, at which time seven were chosen to represent the apostleship, and a number of seventies were chosen. At the conference of 1860, Mr. Smith and his mother, Mrs. Emma Smith, united with them, the speaker joining because directed so to do after appealing in prayer, and he then accepted the platform of the books and pledged himself to teach nothing but what should be approved by them."

In his details of the gospel, he does not name Sts. Marks, Shane and Gurley, these being the founders of the Reorganized Church. The organization was as follows: 1. The above named saints, and a few others, met in solemn prayer before God to see what they should do for salvation. This was in the year 1851, when the spirit of truth, the Holy Ghost, directed to take the book of Doctrine and Covenants for their salvation. 2. One year after this at a public conference, the spirit of truth, the Holy Ghost, changes his first policy and tells them to take the Bible, Book of Mormon and Doc. and Cov. as the groundwork of their salvation. 3. Again the spirit of truth, the Holy Ghost, changes his policy, at a public conference held in 1860, that their plan of salvation was to be the Bible, the B. of M., Doc. and Cov. and an apostolic power represented by seven persons. This is the detailed manner in which the Reorganized Church of Jesus Christ took place, between the years of 1851, and 1860. The church of Marks, Shane and Gurley was organized nine years before the Prophet, Seer and Revealator Jos. Smith became a member of the Reorganized Church. It was in this same year that he pledges himself to be obedient to their confession of faith, the spirit of truth, the Holy Ghost, being his director in answer to prayer. It was then that Joseph Smith placed the massive chain of theological slavery around his neck, by pledging himself to teach nothing but what should be approved by the confession of faith by the Jews, (the Bible) the confession of faith by the Nephites, (the B. of M.) and the confession of faith by the "Mormons," (the Doc. and Cov.) What confidence can we place upon such a changeable mode of salvation?

The salvation of the Lord, the Jesus and the Christ is not the history of the past, the predictions of the future, but the facts of the present embodied in the redemption or gathering of the Zion of God, the Israel of God, the Judah of God and the Gentiles of God.

1. God scattered Joseph, or Zion, by the Ishmaelites. Gen. 37: 28; 49: 22. 2. He scattered the ten tribes of Israel by Solmanezzar, King of Assyria. I. Kings, 14. 3. He scattered Judah by Nebuchadnezzar, King of the Babylonians. Dan. 2. 4. The Lord gave the Holy Ghost to the Gentiles or Romans, which made them mighty in scattering his people at Jerusalem. III. Nephi, 9: Matt. 20: 17.

Paul tells us the scattering of Israel is the salvation of the world, (Rom. 11: 15) abstact and independent of all books; hence, Joseph Smith is wrong in depending on his "Three Book Salvation" and seven representatives of the apostolic power. The Holy Ghost *is* a Spirit of Truth and has but one plan of salvation, and, therefore, could not have allowed a change of faith as one would change his clothing.

The above challenge and article appeared in the *Hearld*, but was not replied to. The following is respectfully ascribed to the limits of extension called Dixion:

"The magitude of your figure to-day is not composed of the same material it was a month ago, you die as fast as you live, every moment subtracts from your existence on earth as much as it adds to it; it mattereth not whether you believe in Moses, Jesus or Mahommed, whether you be a follower of Plato. Cato or Aristotle. The atoms that compose your magnitude shall be transported into a thousand millions of worlds, ten fold as many years will expire before two atoms of your frame will again meet, yet nothing can hinder you from being eternal, though your body be but in atoms. Go on then you holy fugative, you pious rambler, for God shall reward the hellish zeal of a furious bigot, who thinks to please a God and atone for his sin by trampling upon law, liberty and the lives of those who do not believe as he does. The time is near for the end of all such on this planet.

As a free born Scotchman, I, of my own free choice, adopted the Constitution of America, because of my love for the liberty of thought, the freedom of speach and the liberty of the press therein guaranteed; but now it is plain to be seen by every honest man that, Whigery has become a "clickery" of popularity, by giving the unsettled regions of the country in government grants to canal and railroad monopolies; and should the honest man, black, white or red, exhibit a better title, yet the railroad and canal companies know full well that every statesman, lawier and judge has his price, therefore the Constitution is trampled under their feet.

"The rights and authorities reserved to the states and territories and to the people, as equally incorporated with, and essential to the success, of the general system; to avoid the slightest interference with the rights of conscience, or the functions of religion, so wisely exempted from civil jurisdiction; to preserve in their full energy, the other salutary provisions in behalf of private and personal rights, and of the freedom of the press; as far as intention aids in the fulfillment of duty, are consumations too big with benefits not to captivate the energies of all honest men to achieve them, when they can be brought to pass by reciprocation, friendly alliances, wise legeslation and honorable treties.

The government has once flourished under the guidance of trusty servants; and Hon. Mr. Monroe in his day, while speaking of the Constitution; says, 'states respectively protected by the national government, under a mild paternal system, against foreign dangers, and enjoying within their separate spheres, a just proportion of the sovreignty, have extended their settlements, and attained a strength and maturity which are the best proofs of wholesome law well administered. And, if we look to the condition of individuals, what a proud specticle to see a nation composed of nations and all protected in religious liberty."

Elder Erastus Snow, at conference April 4, 1881, said: "The time will come when the voice of such men as will undermine the fabric of freedom and break down the guarantees of human liberty that God has established in their endeavors to oppress the people of God and destroy the institutions of heaven out of the earth—the voice of such men will be heard in the land like the roaring of a tornado, so that the still small voice speaking from the heavens cannot be heard; and the voice of the loud mouth, plotting destruction to human liberty will be heard all over the land, and everybody raise up and say, it is the voice of God; and they will be willing to stand and look on and see the *Saints butchered* and *Prophets martyred* and our institutions wasted away. But when that time comes, the Lord will come forth from his hiding place and 'vex the nations;' he will raise his arm and it shall not be turned back, and he will stay the hand raised against his people to destroy them and their institutions.

The gospel has been the means of gathering us out from among the nations and has made us a free and happy people, an able and united commonwealth; and the Lord is using us to establish its principles in these mountains, *that throuhout these valleys may be formed a nucleus around which honorable men and women may gather*, men who will be capable of appreciating the blessings of liberty and of helping to extend them to others. And all presidents and senators and judges and all men in official authority who shall lend themselves and their influence to trample upon the common rights of man, those rights which God has bestowed upon us and which are our common heritage, and who shall be found warring against God and his institutions, when the cup of their iniquity shall be full, the Lord Almighty will cause them to disappear from the public gaze; he will let them sink into oblivion and disgrace."

Thus sayeth the "Angel of the Prairies" in 1845, "'Behold a century cometh, etc.' Is it possible that a republic founded upon the most liberal principles, and established by the sweat and blood and tears of our renowned ancestors, and so cherished by their children, has faded like the dazzling splendor of the mornings dawn? has withered like an untimely flower? and that, too, by the corruptions of its own degenerate sons, the very persons who should have cherished it forever ? Where was the spirit of patriotism, of freedom, of love of country which had once characterised the sons of liberty, and warmed the bossoms of Americans?

Although their had been great corruption and a general overthrow of our government and its institutions, yet many of the sons of noble sires had stood firm and unshaken in the cause of freedom; even amid the wreck of states and the crash of thrones, they had maintained their integrity, and when they had no longer a country or government to fight for, they retired to the plains of the West, carrying with them the pure spirit of freedom. There in the midst of a more extensive, a richer and a better country they had established a better government more permanent, strong and lasting, and vastly more extensive and glorious, combining strength and solidity, with the most perfect liberty and freedom. Nor had their labors been confined to the narrow limits of their own immediate country and nation, but had burst the chains of tyrany and broken the yoke of bondage from the growing millions of all nations and colors; and where darkness, ignorance, superstition, cruelty and bloodshed had held dominion for ages, light had sprung up, truth had tryumphed, and peace had commenced its universal reign. And where, a century ago, an extensive and fertile country lay desolate and lone, or partially occupied by ignorant and cruel savages, hundreds of millions of intelligent and happy beings were now enjoying all the sweets of domestic felicity.

The only perfect system of government is a theocracy; that is, a government under the immediate, constant and direct superintendency of the Almighty. This order of government commenced in Eden, when God chose Adam for a ruler and gave him laws. It was perpetuated in his descendents, such as Seth, Enoch, Noah, Melchisedec, and so on, till it came down to Abraham, and was made hereditary in his seed forever. As it is written, 'Kings shall be of thee, and princes shall come out of thy loins.'

It was manifested clearly in Egypt—Pharaoh himself being instructed and governed by Joseph, as a revelator. Moses also delivered a nation from slavery, dethroned a tyrant, and governed in all things by these same principles. By these Joshua conquered, the Judges ruled. By this authority Samuel reproved and displaced a corrupted priesthood, in the case of Eli and his sons; by it he annoints King Saul to reign in Israel, and by it he afterwards rejected him for transgression and annointed David in his stead. By this authority Elijah reproved and rejected Ahab and the priests of Baal, and then proceeded to annoint Jehu king and Elisha for prophet and by this means remodeled the civil and religious administration of affairs, and saved a nation from the lowest depths of corruption and ruin. By this power Daniel reproved and instructed Nebuchadnezzar, displaced Beltshazzar and directed Cyrus; continually impressing upon kings and nations this one important principle; viz., 'that God is a revealer of secrets, and claims the right of government over kings and potentates of the earth.' To convince Nebuchadnezzar of this one fact, he was driven out from his throne and from the society of men, to dwell among the beasts of the field and to eat grass as the ox, and afterwards restored to his kingdom again. And to convince all nations of this fact, King Nebuchadnezzar wrote his epistle to all nations and languages, in which he bore testimony to the same.

By this Authority Jesus Christ received all power in heaven and on the earth, and was therefore seen by Daniel, coming in the clouds of heaven, to reign over all the earth. By this authority His Apostles governed those who would receive His Kingdom in their day—being themselves chosen by the Lord, and not by the people. By this same authority the Gentile Church and people would have been governed from that day to the present, without a schism or division of church or state, were it not for corruption and wickedness, which made war with the Saints, and overcame them, and changed times and laws, as was foretold by the prophet Daniel.

By this authority the God of heaven promised, by all the holy prophets, that He would set up a Kingdom that should destroy and break in pieces all these kingdoms, become universal, and stand forever. And that He would do this by the sitting of the Ancient of Days, whose raiment was white as snow, and whose hair was like the pure wool; while thousands of thousands ministered unto him, ten thousand times ten thousand stood before him, and judgment was given to the Saints, and the time came that the Saints possessed the Kingdom.

By this authority the God of heaven has fulfilled that which He spoke by the mouths of His ancient prophets, by revealing from heaven and appointing and establishing a glorious Kingdom which shall stand forever.

Son of mortal, you now understand the nature of the government you have beheld. You see it is not a human monarchy, for man-made kings are tyrants. It is not an aristocracy, for in that case the few trample upon the rights of many. It is not a democracy, for mobs composed of the mass, with no stronger power to check them, are the greatest tyrants and oppressors in the world. But it is a theocracy, where the great Eloheim, Jehovah, holds the superior honor. He selects the officers. He reveals and appoints the laws, and He counsels, reproves, directs, guides and holds the reins of government. The venerable Council which you beheld enthroned in majesty and clad in robes of white, with crowns upon their heads, is the order of the

Ancient of Days, before whose august presence thrones have been cast down, and tyrants have ceased to rule. You have understood the secret purposes of Providence in relation to the prairies and the West, and of the earth and its destiny. Go forth on your journey, and wander no more; but tell the world of things to come."

The House of God being set in order, the Ancient of Days having finished his work, he hands it over to the Savoir, our Lord Jesus Christ. The following is from the vision of '100 years hence' *Mill. Star*, Vol. 6, page 140:

"Now the eyes of our understanding began to be quickened, and we learned that we were 100 years ahead of common life, and we glorified. The 'veil' that hides our view from the glory of the upper deep had been taken away, and all things appeared to us as to the Lord. The great earthquake mentioned by John had leveled the mountains over the whole earth:—the sea had rolled back as it was in the beginning, the crooked was made straight, and the rough places plain. The earth yielded her increase, and the knowledge of God exalted man to the society of resurrected beings. The melody and prayer of the morning in Zion showed, that the *"Lord was there,"* and truly so; for, after breakfast the chariot of Jesus Christ was made ready for a pleasure ride; and the chariots of his "144,000" glittered in the setineau of earty's greatest and best, so gloriously, that the show exhibited the splendor of *gods*, whose Father's name they bore on the front of their crowns."

"Death and Satan being banished;
And the 'veil' forever vanished;
All the earth 's again replenished,
 And in beauty appears:
So we'll sing hallelujah's.
While we worship our Savior,
And fill the earth with cities
Through the 'great thousand years.'"

PROPHETIC NUMBERS.

Prophetic time.	Continuous years.	Prophetic Incidents.	Date of incident	After decree
weeks	years	Decree to rebuild walls of Jerusalem.	B. C. 400	years
62	434	to Crucifixion.	A D 34	434
7	49	to Destruction of J.	79	483
70½ weeks	495 end.	to Going of woman into the wilderness.	574	978
days.	years.	Taking Man-child.	544	948
	30	to going of Woman.	574	978
1260	1230	birth of Man-child.	1805	2208
		1st Woe begins.	1820	2223
1290	30	Restoration.	1835	2238
		2nd Woe begins.	1862	2265
1335	45	Year of Jubilee.	1880	2283
56	12	Winding up Scene.	1891	2295
2300	5	Sanctuary cleansed	1896	2300
70	8	Gospel to Gentiles.	1905	2308
		3rd Woe begins.	1905	2308
100	39	Restitution of peace	1945	2347

How long should the Sanctuary and the Host be trodden under foot of the Gentiles? 2300 years.
What year did the vision begin? 400 B. C.
What year did the 62 weeks end? 34 A. D.
When was Jerusalem destroyed? 79 "
When did the whole 139½ weeks end? 574 "
When was the man-child taken to God? 544 "
How long was the man-child with God? 1260 years.
How long was the woman in wilderness? 1260 years.
What time did Daniel's 1290 ds cover?- 544 to 1834.
" " " 1335 " 544 to 1879.
When should the scene of persecution wind up? 1891.
When should the 2300 days be fulfilled? 1896.
When will the 70 years of Jeremiah end? 1904.
When will be the restitution of peace on earth and good will to man and city of Zion be built? 1945.

www.ingramcontent.com/pod-product-compliance
Lightning Source LLC
Chambersburg PA
CBHW030310170426
43202CB00009B/953